WordWork Book

Volume 2, Units 9–16

Maryanne Wolf

2 3 4 5 6 BNG 15 14 13 12 11

ISBN-13: 978-1-60697-469-8
ISBN-10: 1-60697-469-6

279380/1-11

Printed in the United States of America
Published and Distributed by

4093 Specialty Place • Longmont, Colorado 80504
(303) 651-2829 • www.soprislearning.com

Contents

Unit 9 Duck Luck

Unit 12 Jack on the Track

Unit 14 Bones

Unit 15 The Chopper

Unit 16 What Is in the Cave?

Name ______________________

Create *deck*

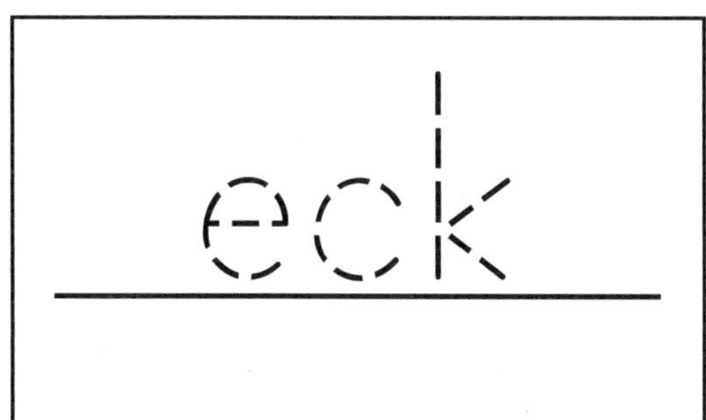

Bob sets the pot on the __________.

Name ______________________

Dictated Phrases *deck* and *neck*

1. ____

____

2. ____

____

3. ____

____

Name ______________________

Create *well*

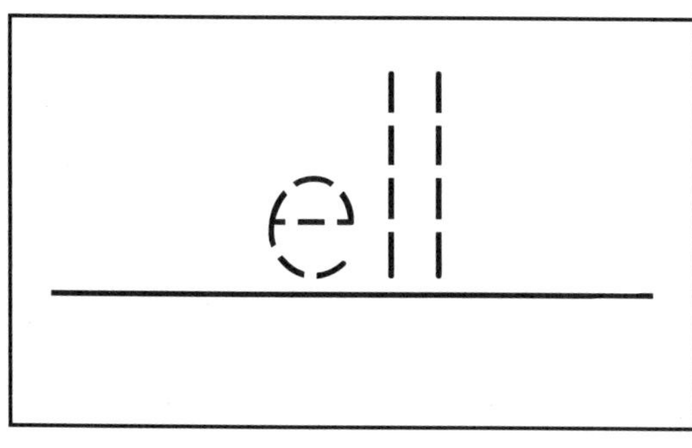

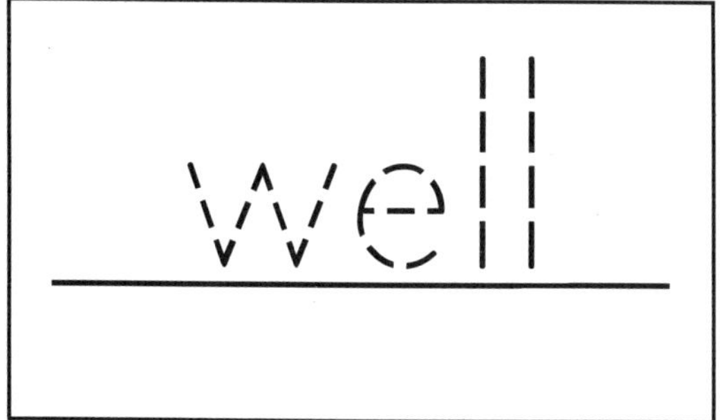

I am just not ____________.

Name ______________________

Dictated Phrases *well* and *bell*

1. ____

____

2. ____

____

3. ____

____

Name ____________________

Rime Family Words

Real Words	Non-Words

Write your sentence here:

____

____

Name ____________________

Create *bed*

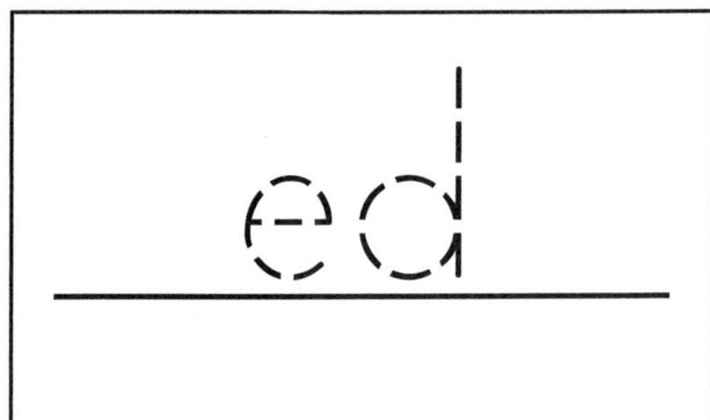

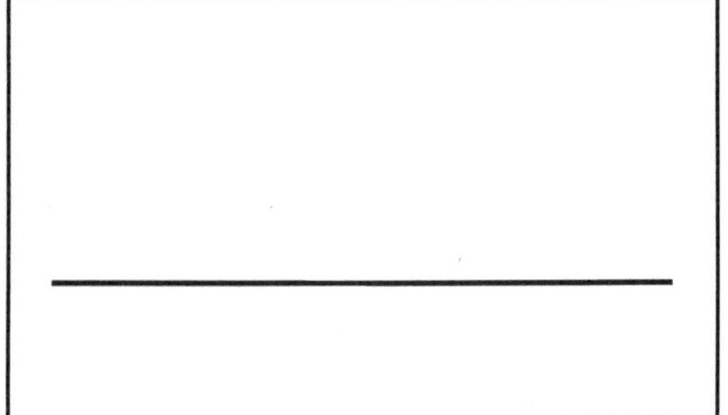

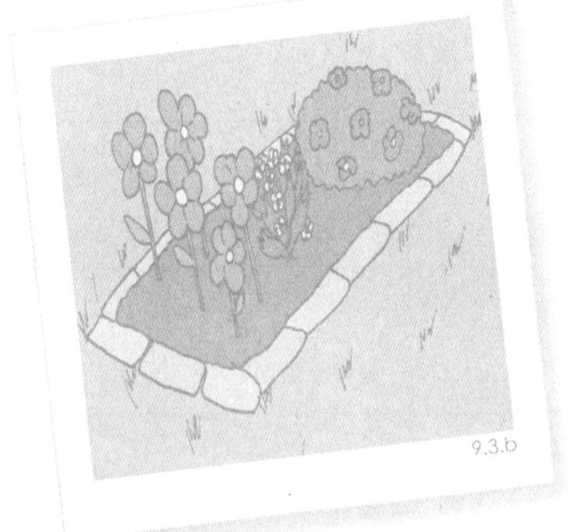

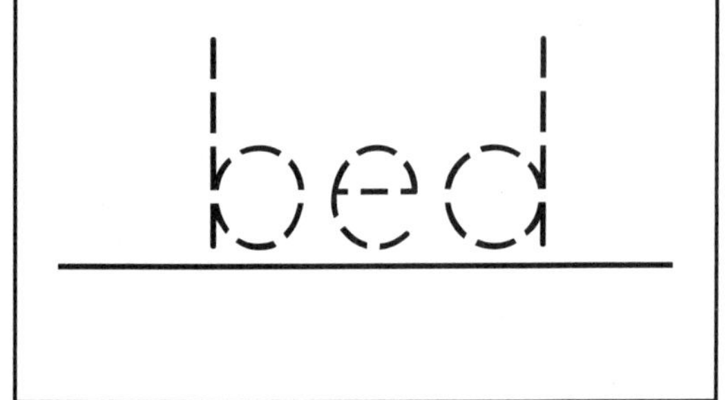

Are you set for __________?

Name ______________________

Dictated Phrases *bed* and *red*

1. ______________________________

____

2. ______________________________

____

3. ______________________________

____

Name ____________________

Create *pen*

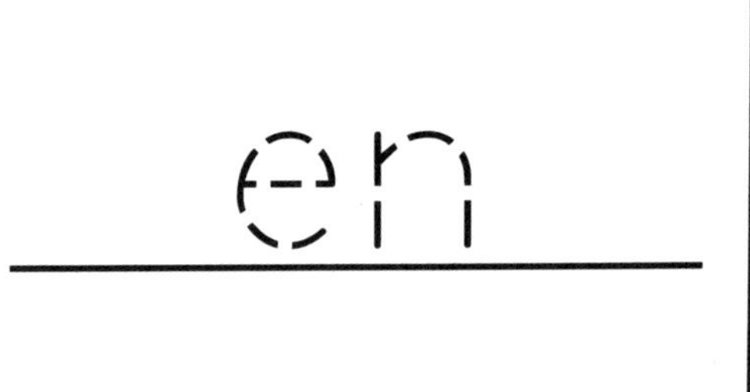

9.4.c

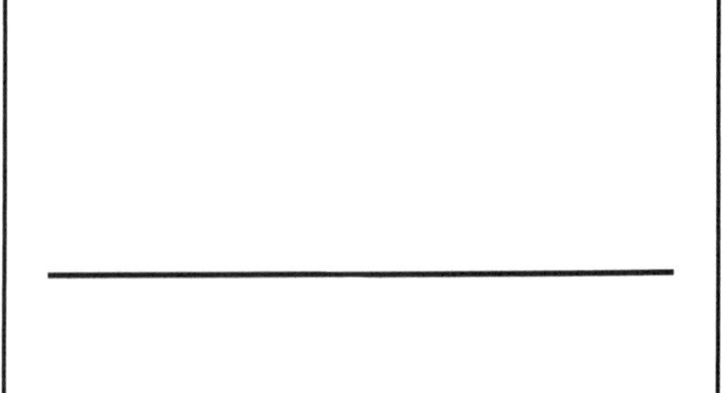

9.4.a

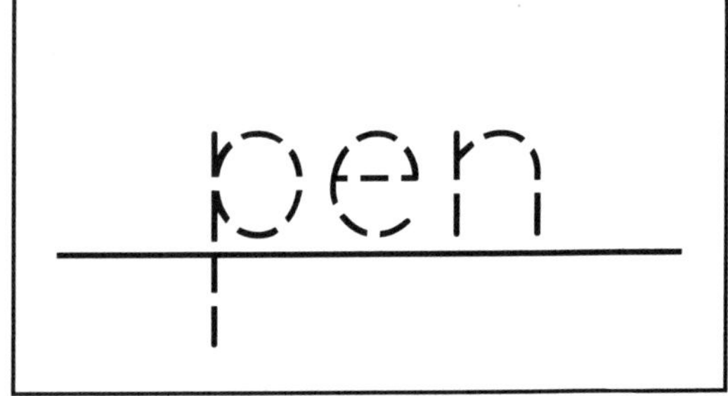

9.4.b

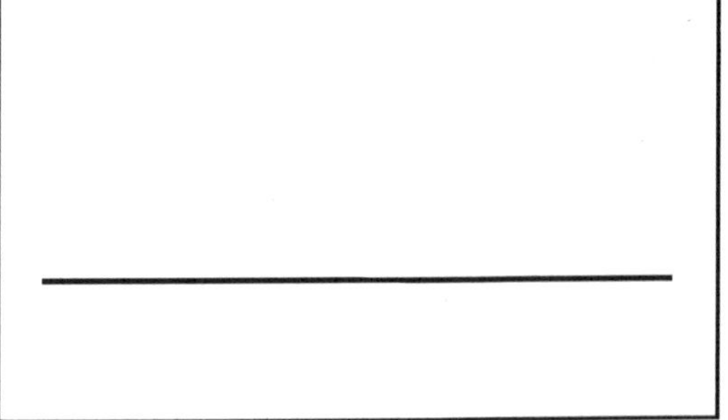

The pig is in the ____________.

Name ______________________

Dictated Phrases *pen* and *ten*

1. ____

____

2. ____

____

3. ____

____

Name ______________________________

Eye-Spy Words

Units 2–8

the	do	I	get	that
is	on	are	from	me
in	not	of	what	out
a	see	he	my	but
this	at	by	was	so
and	it	with	little	Mom
has	she	for	him	then
	his	to	we	up
	happy	said	if	

____

____

____

____

____

____

Name ____________________

Question Sentences

Question words: ***when, what, where, why, who***

1. __________ can I go to the lock?
(When, What)

2. __________ is the little boy going to?
(Why, Where)

3. __________ is Mom so happy?
(Who, Why)

4. __________ can I do?
(What, Where)

5. __________ is that fanning with a fan?
(When, Who)

Write your own sentence using any of the question words.

____

____

Name ______________________

Create *pet*

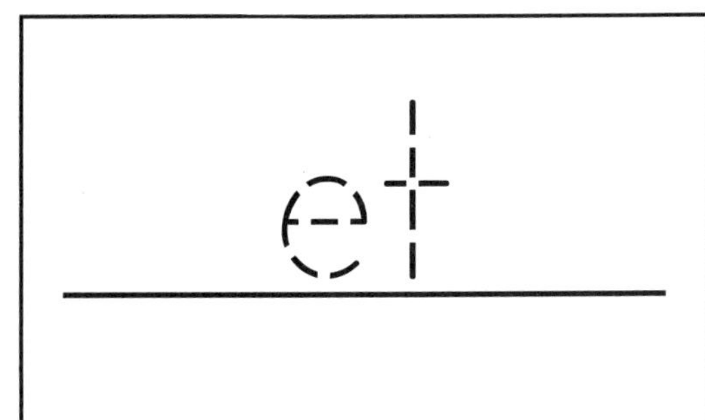

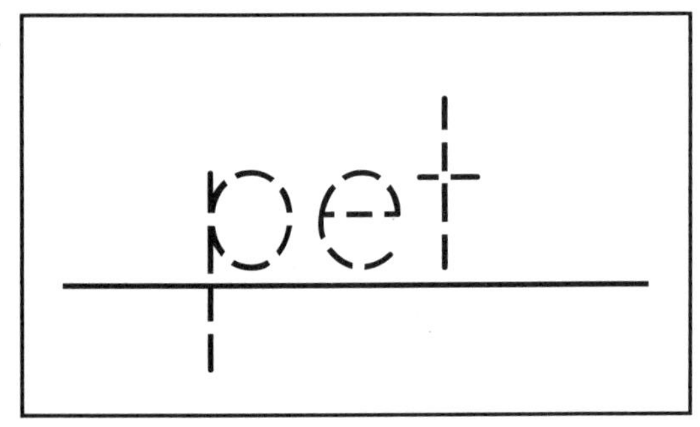

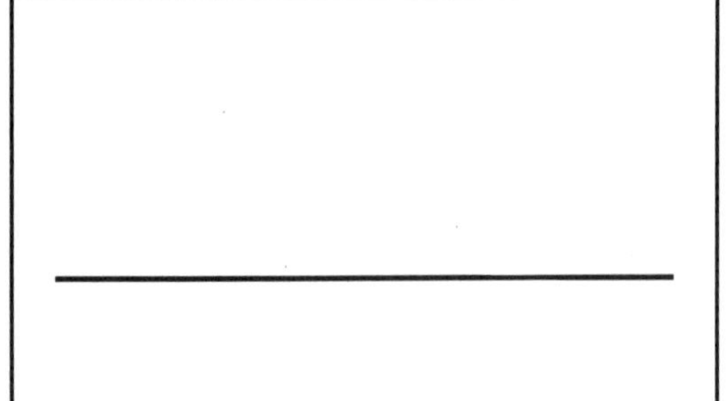

9.5.a

9.5.b

__________ the pig in the pen!

Name ______________________

Dictated Phrases *pet* and *set*

1. ______________________________

____

2. ______________________________

____

3. ______________________________

____

Name ______________________

Create *leg*

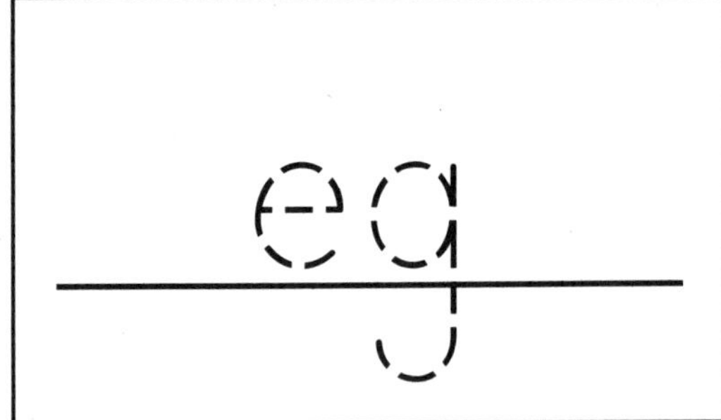

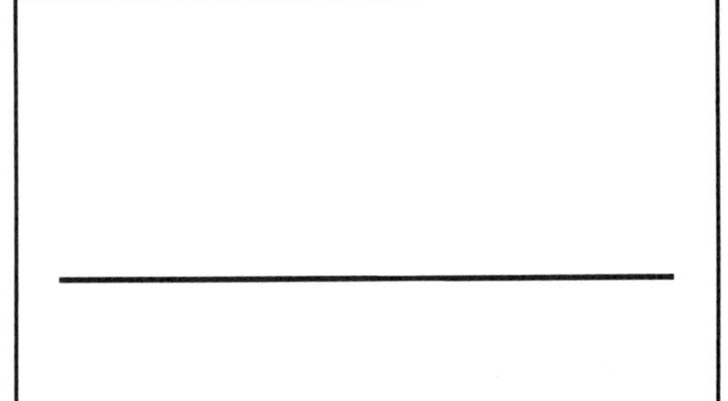

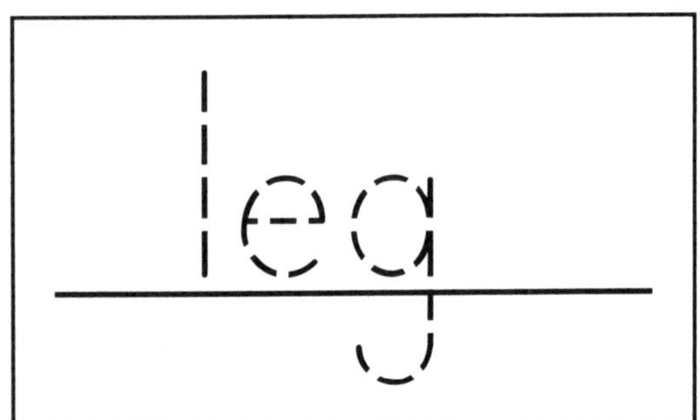

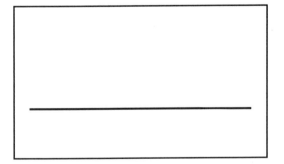

The man has a bad __________.

UNIT 9

Name ____________________

Dictated Phrases *leg* and *beg*

1. ____

____

2. ____

____

3. ____

____

Name ______________________

"Ted Gets Sick"

Ted is not well. He is getting sick, and he is upset. His mom says Ted must not get out of his sickbed.

How did Ted get sick? Ted has a "bug." It is not a bug that you can see. If you get this bug, you can get sick!

The bad bug bugs Ted.
How can Ted get better?

Ted gets very, very hot and very red. Ted gets hotter and redder, and then the bad bug gets unwell! Getting very hot zaps the bug!

Ted sips a lot of water. Ted naps and naps in his bed.

His mom can see that he is getting better.

Ted is well! The bug is not bugging him, so Ted is better!

Time taken:

2nd reading ____________ 2nd reading ____________ 3rd reading ____________

Name ______________________

Ticket Out the Door

The bell fell in the wishing well.

The deck is on a bed of rocks.

Is the duck on the dock or the deck?

The man in the bed is not well.

Name ____________________

Rime Pattern Worksheet

See how many words you can make with these rimes in one minute.

at	et	it	ot	ut

Name ______________________

"Duck Luck"

The man was on the dock. He was upset. He had no luck in getting a fish.

A duck dipped his neck by the dock. Zip! Zap! The duck bobbed up with a fish in his bill.

"You are mocking me," said the man. "I cannot get a fish from the lock. I am in a rut. I am not fit to fish!"

With a sob, he lobbed his fishnet. As the net fell, it nicked the gills and fins of lots of fish. The net filled with fish.

The man tugged the net up. Fish fell onto the dock, wet and fat. The man picked them up and set them in his bag.

The bag sagged. "Well," said the man, "I am fit to fish."

The duck dipped his neck but got no fish.

The man set a big, red fish on the dock for the duck. "You are in luck, duck," the man said, "and so am I!"

Time taken:

2nd reading ____________ 2nd reading ____________ 3rd reading ____________

Name ______________________

RAN Chart (Core Words)

deck	well	bed	pet
leg	pen	deck	pet
bed	well	leg	pen

Time taken:

2nd reading ____________ 2nd reading ____________ 3rd reading ____________

Name ______________________

Pet Shop List

Check (✓) the things you can get at a pet shop.

___ **1.** a cat's bed

___ **2.** a little bell

___ **3.** a fishing rod

___ **4.** a wishing well

___ **5.** a red pen

___ **6.** a set of pans

___ **7.** a rubber duck

___ **8.** a bag of nuts

___ **9.** a water jet

___ **10.** a bill from the vet

UNIT 9

Name ______________________

Ender Benders Worksheet

Work through the sentences, highlighting the correct words for each sentence. Some correct words will have Ender Benders, but some will not.

1. I can see two (well, wells, welling).
2. Pat is not (well, wells, welling).
3. The (deck, decks, decked) is red.
4. The man is (decks, decking) out his (deck, decked).
5. The cat has little (legs, legging, legged).
6. Pam hit her (legged, legging, leg) on the rock.
7. Bob is (pet, pets, petting, petted) his cat.
8. Where are the (pet, pets, petting, petted) fish?
9. I (penned, pens) the rams in the big (pen, penning).
10. Nick has a big red (pen, pens, penning, penned).
11. I must go to (bed, beds, bedding, bedded).
12. Tuck the (bedding, bedded) in the (bed, bedded).

Name ______________________

"Can I See the Sunset?"

Where will the sun set?
Here by the mill?

They are running
to the top of the hill!

When can I go?
Who must I tell?
Mom says,
"Just sit by the well."

"Why not sit here
just for fun?
What can you see?"
"It is the sun."

"You can see the dell.
The dell is sunlit."
The dell gets redder,
just for a bit.

THEN...
There is no sun!
The sun has set!

Time taken:

2nd reading ____________ 2nd reading ____________ 3rd reading ____________

Name ______________________________

RAN Chart (Core Words + Review)

can	kick	deck	pet
nut	well	lap	cap
bed	tap	pen	leg

Time taken:

2nd reading ____________ 2nd reading ____________ 3rd reading ____________

Name ____________________

Build Rime Family Words

Real Words	Non-Words

Name ______________________________

Make a Word Web

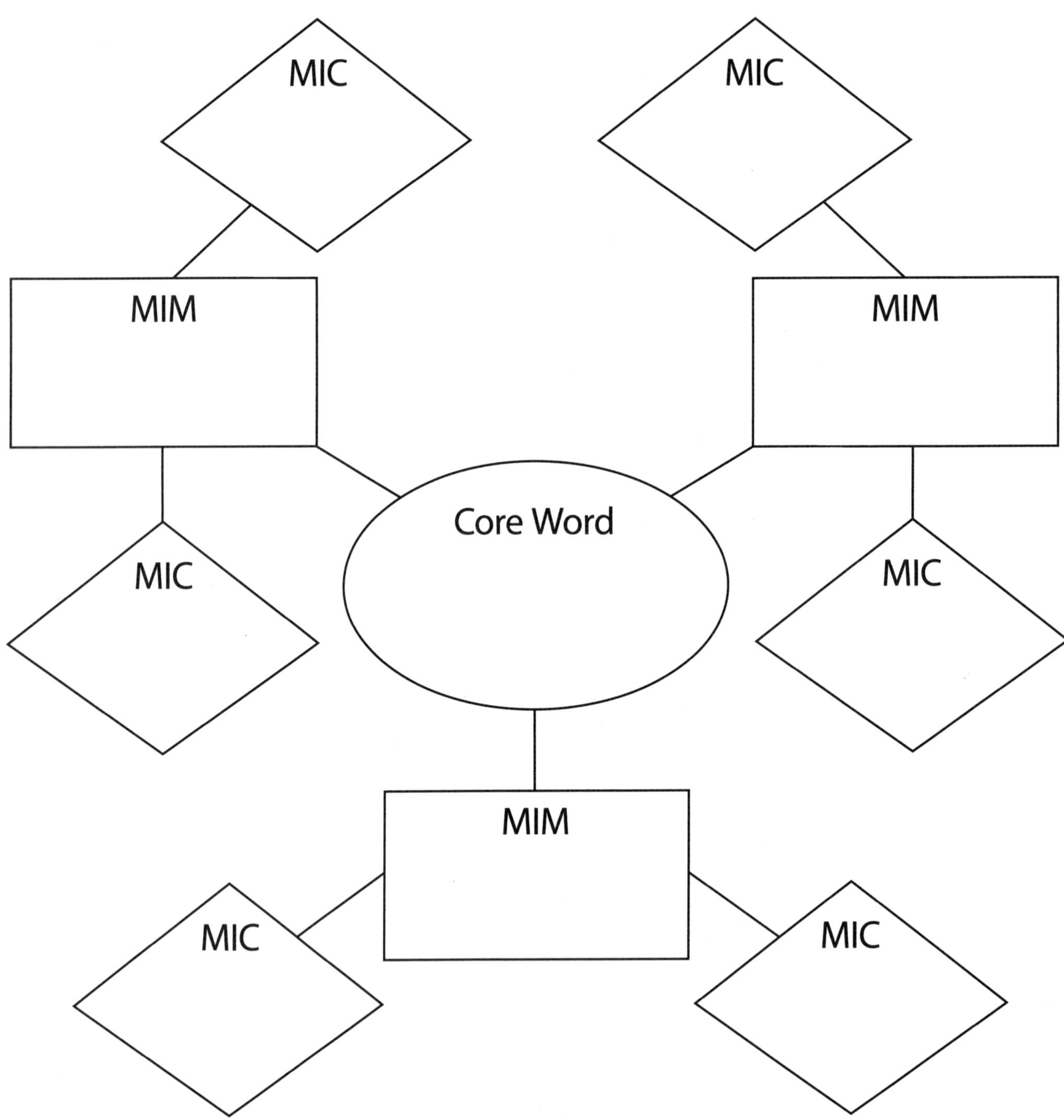

UNIT 9 Name ____________________

Sam Sleuth Worksheet

1. Starts with ***b***, similar to ***insect***	bun	bag	bug	bust
2. Starts with ***t***, similar to a ***label***	tap	tag	top	tip
3. Starts with ***l***, sounds like ***sock***	lick	lip	lap	lock
4. Starts with ***j***, sounds like ***rust***	jam	Jill	just	job
5. Sounds like ***sill***, starts with ***b***	bill	bag	bit	bob
6. Sounds like ***wish***, starts with ***d***	dip	dot	dock	dish
7. Sounds like ***bell***, starts with ***w***	will	dell	hill	well
8. Sounds like ***tap***, starts with ***l***	lap	lip	lag	lock
9. Similar to ***hit***, sounds like ***mat***	cat	pat	sat	hat
10. Similar to ***hat***, sounds like ***lap***	map	lap	nap	cap
11. Similar to ***pan***, sounds like ***hot***, starts with ***p***	pot	pin	pat	pip

Name ____________________

er Worksheet

Person	More	Pretender Bender Word

UNIT 9

Name ______________________

Word Wall

pad		kick		bob	rub	deck	
tag		kid		lock			
jam		dig		rock	duck		
ham		pig				bed	
ram		bill			bug	leg	
can		pin		top		well	
fan		dip		pop			
cap		tip			run	pen	
lap		fish				pet	
tap		bit		pot	just		
bat					nut		
pat							

Time taken:

2nd reading ____________ 2nd reading ____________ 3rd reading ____________

Name ____________________

Ender Bender *ed* Worksheet

End Sound *d*	End Sound *t*	End Sound *ed* (as in *Ted*)

UNIT 9 Name ____________________

"Mom Sees a Martian"

Mom was napping in the sun in her rocker on the dock. Mom sat up and rubbed her eyes.

A little man popped up out of a copper pod on the dock.

"I must be sick," Mom said. "I can see a little man!"

"I am a Martian," he said. "The top of my pod has ripped, and a bit is jutting out. What can I do?"

The little man patted the top of the copper pod. "This bit is sagging. I cannot fit it."

Mom picked up the top and tugged it. She fitted it on the pod.

"I am so happy," said the little Martian.

He got into the pod. Zip, zap, the pod was a dot in the dust.

Mom sat in her rocker and rubbed her eyes. Was she unwell or was she just napping?

Time taken:

2nd reading ____________ 2nd reading ____________ 3rd reading ____________

Name ______________________________

RAN Chart

hop to the top	leg of the bed	the big dig
nut at the top	sit on the lap	can the jam
run the laps	pen and pad	just kick a bit
the rock rocks	hip-hop fan	just the job

Time taken:

2nd reading ____________ 2nd reading ____________ 3rd reading ____________

Name ______________________

Write Rime Family Words

Sentence 1:

Sentence 2:

Name ___________________________

Sam Sleuth Game

1.
Which are the nouns in this sentence?
Pop had his rock in the top of his locker.

2.
What is the helping verb in this sentence?
Nick can tap the bill of his cap.

3.
Which words are the pronouns in this sentence?
We hit it to her.

4. Which words are describers in this sentence?
The madcap robber tipped the big van.

5.
What is the helping verb in this sentence?
I am napping!

6.
What are the action verbs in this sentence?
Nick can tip and dip.

7.
Name a Fatrat word and put it in a sentence.

8.
Write a noun + verb + noun sentence.

9.
Add ender bender ***ing*** to "fish" and use it in a sentence.

Name ______________________

Sam Sleuth Game Answer Sheet

1. ______________________

2. ______________________

3. ______________________

4. ______________________

5. ______________________

6. ______________________

7. ______________________

____

8. ______________________

____

9. ______________________

____

Name ______________________

Create *cane*

ane

cane

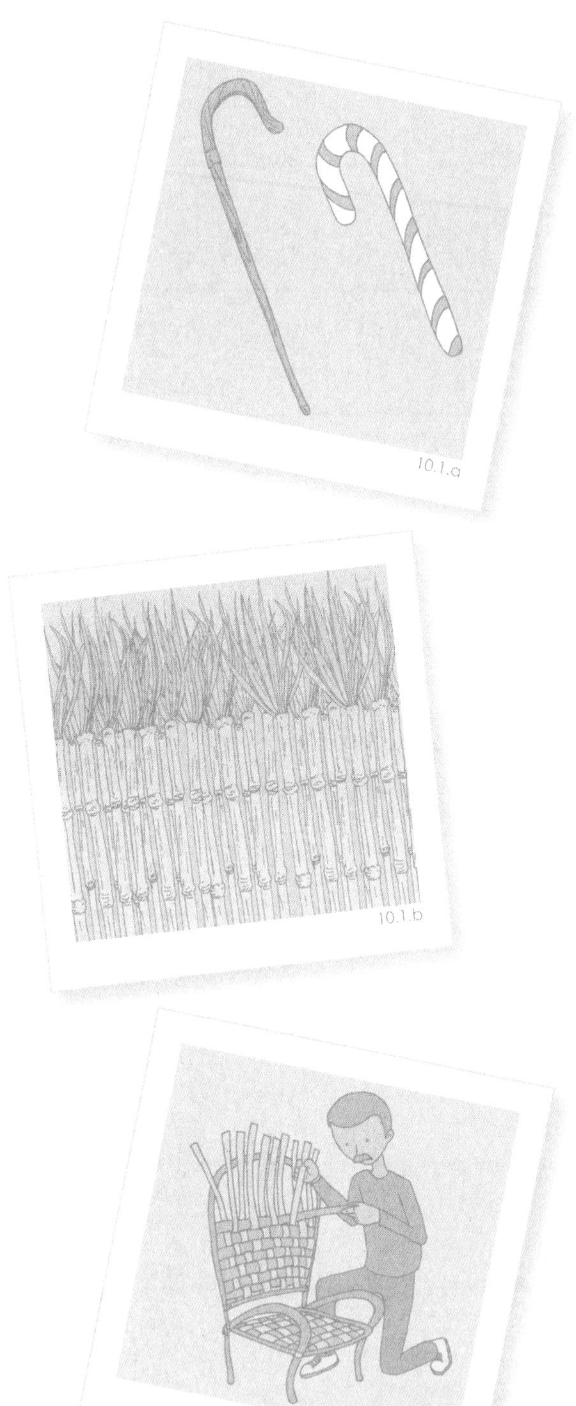

The man has a ______________.

Name ______________________

Dictated Phrases *cane* and *lane*

1. ____

____

2. ____

____

3. ____

____

Name ______________________

Create *date*

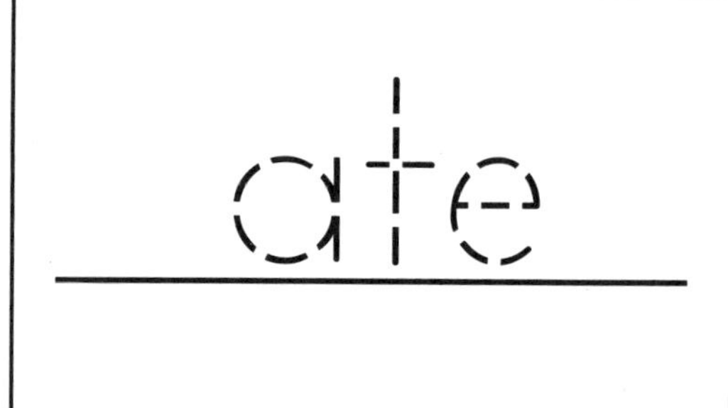

10.2.c

10.2.d

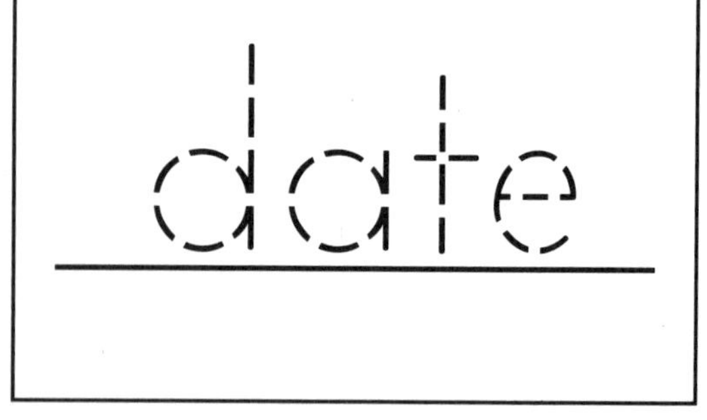

10.2.a

What ______________ is our ______________?

Name ______________________

Dictated Phrases *date* and *late*

1. ______________________

____

2. ______________________

____

3. ______________________

____

Name ______________________

Create *cape*

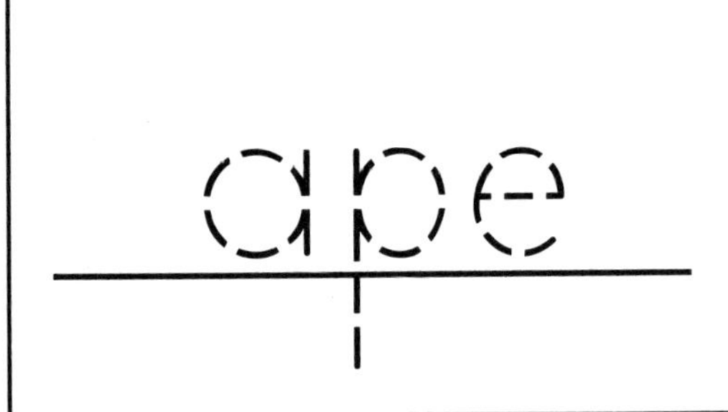

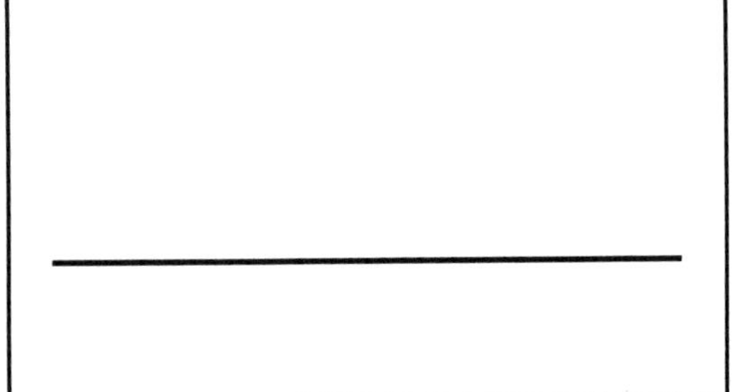

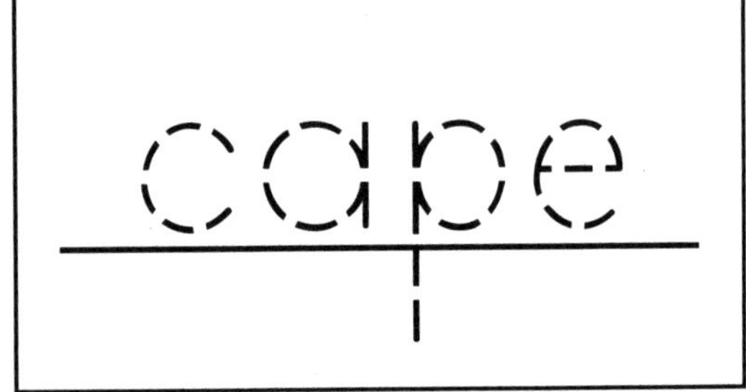

I live on ______________ Cod.

Name ____________________

Dictated Phrases *cape* and *tape*

1. ____________________

____

2. ____________________

____

3. ____________________

____

UNIT 10

Name ______________________

Rime Family Words

				at
				ate
				an
				ane
				ap
				ape

Name ______________________

Create *pine*

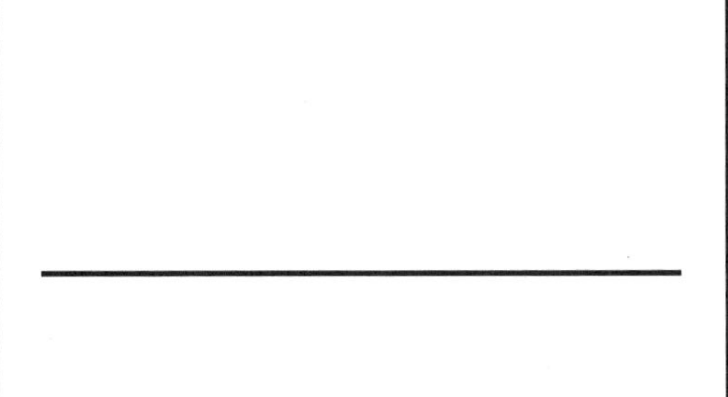

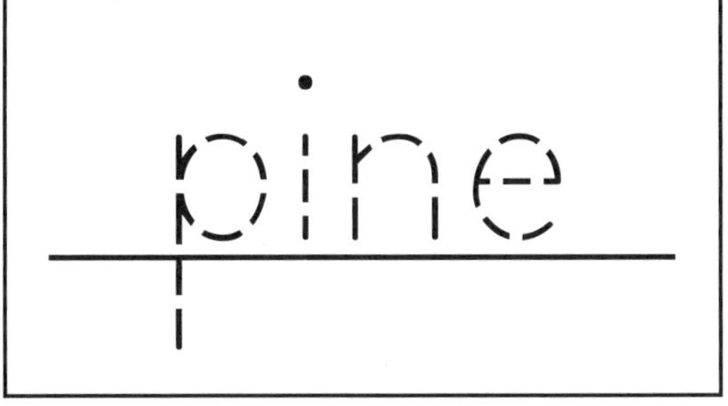

Sam sat by the ______________.

Name ______________________

Create *fine*

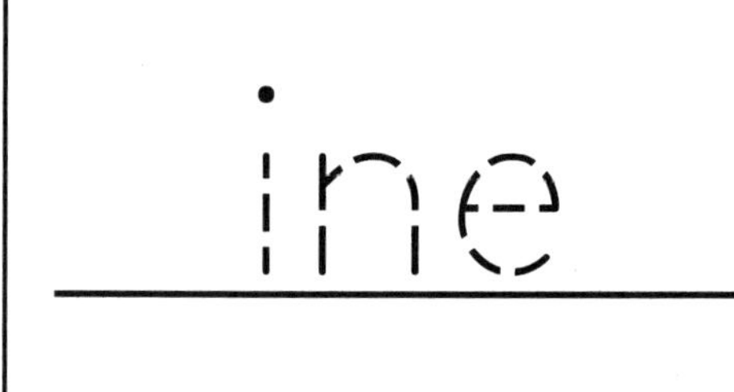

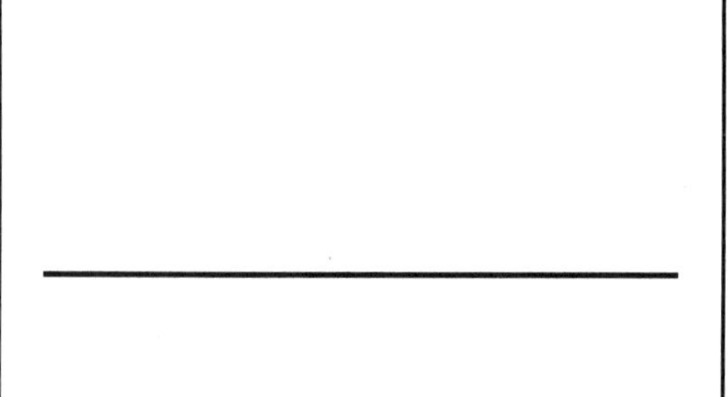

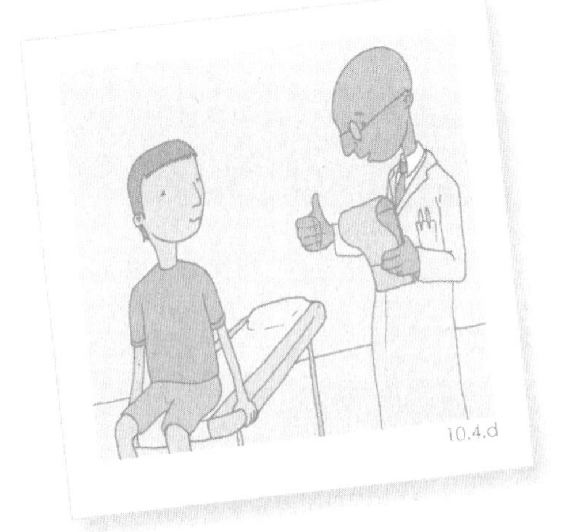

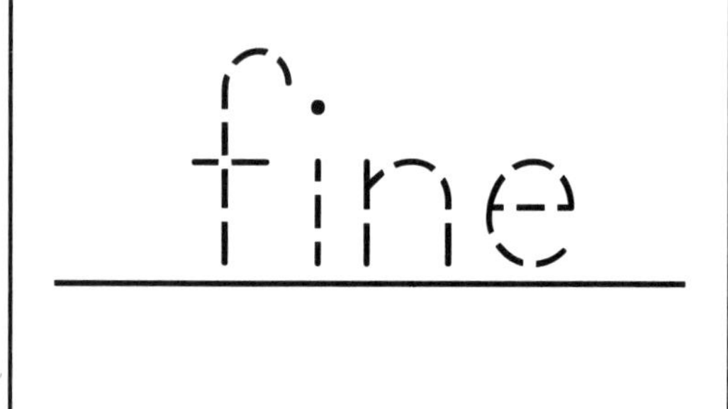

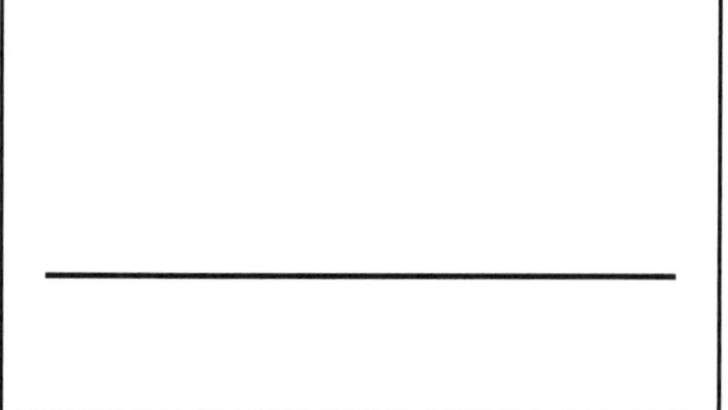

Did he get a ______________?

Name ______________________

Dictated Phrases *pine* and *fine*

1. ____

____

2. ____

____

3. ____

____

Name ______________________

Writing Sentences

1. ____

____

2. ____

____

3. ____

____

4. ____

____

Name ______________________

CVC*e* and Ender Bender *s*

Write the words shown in parenthesis on the blank lines and put Ender Bender ***s*** on them if they need it. Circle if the word is used as a noun or a verb in the sentence.

1. The man likes the van in the ____________.
(lane)

noun or ***verb***

2. Zapcat has 2 ____________.
(cape)

noun or ***verb***

3. Jill has ten big ____________ in the van.
(cane)

noun or ***verb***

4. Jen ____________ for her dog.
(pine)

noun or ***verb***

5. Top Cop ____________ and locks up the robber.
(fine)

noun or ***verb***

Name ____________________

Eye-Spy Words

Units 2–9

the	do	I	get	that	when	as
is	on	are	from	me	why	them
in	not	of	what	out	where	go
a	see	he	my	but	who	they
this	at	by	was	so	how	here
and	it	with	little	Mom	very	there
has	she	for	him	then	water	
	his	to	we	up	says	
	happy	said	if		you	
					no	

Name ____________________

"Jane's Kite"

It is hot, and Jane wants to have fun in the sun.

She makes a kite.
She makes it with pipes, tape, and a very big cape.

She cuts a line and cuts the cape.
She tapes the line to the cape and the cape to the pipes.

Jane likes her kite! It is a fine kite.
She runs with her kite. The kite dips and bobs.

Pat sees Jane and her kite.

"That is a fine kite," says Pat.
"Can I tug the kite with my bike?"

The bike zips and zags with the kite.
Jane and Pat like this game a lot.

Time taken:

2nd reading ____________ 2nd reading ____________ 3rd reading ____________

Name ______________________

RAN Chart (Core Words)

cape	date	cane	fine
pine	date	pine	cape
fine	cane	cape	date

Time taken:

2nd reading ____________ 2nd reading ____________ 3rd reading ____________

Name ______________________

RAN Chart (Core Words + Review)

cane	pin	cape	can
pine	date	cane	deck
cane	leg	cape	bed
fine	can	pine	cap

Time taken:

2nd reading ____________ 2nd reading ____________ 3rd reading ____________

Name ______________________

Long Vowel or Short Vowel?

Magic-*e*	No Magic-*e*
______	______
______	______
______	______
______	______
______	______
______	______
______	______
______	______

Name ____________________

"Zapcat's Date"

The date is 2-14-09, a fine time for going on a date.

Then he gets a call from Cape Cod from his fan, the man in the van.

Zapcat tells his date that he must go to the man in the van.

He is at the beck and call of all who are in a jam.

Zapcat picks up his cape, tucks the cape tapes in his hands, and jets off.

Zapcat zips by the tall pines to get to the man in the van.

Zapcat sees the man and his van pinned by a big grapevine.

"You were in the nick of time," said the man.
"I must say, this is a fine jam," said Zapcat.
"Well!" said the man. "We can say this is a grape jam!"

Time taken:

2nd reading ____________ 2nd reading ____________ 3rd reading ____________

Name ______________________

Magic-*e* Rime Patterns and Words

Starters: ***t, d, c, c, c, k, p, p, f***

ap	it	ip
at	ap	in
in	an	am

Time taken:

2nd reading ____________ 2nd reading ____________ 3rd reading ____________

UNIT 10 Name ____________________

Write Words With Magic-*e* and Ender Bender *s*

Choose the correct word inside each ( ) and write it on the blank line.

1. The two __________ are on the __________.
   (hats, hates) (lin, line)

2. The __________ are in the red __________.
   (dat, dates) (can, cane)

3. My __________ is __________.
   (cats, cat) (fin, fine)

4. The __________ nuts are in the __________.
   (pin, pine) (lan, lane)

5. I am __________ for the __________ at the dig.
   (lat, late) (dat, date)

6. He ________ the ________ nut on the ________.
   (pin, pins) (pine, pines) (hate, hat)

Name ____________________

Create *note*

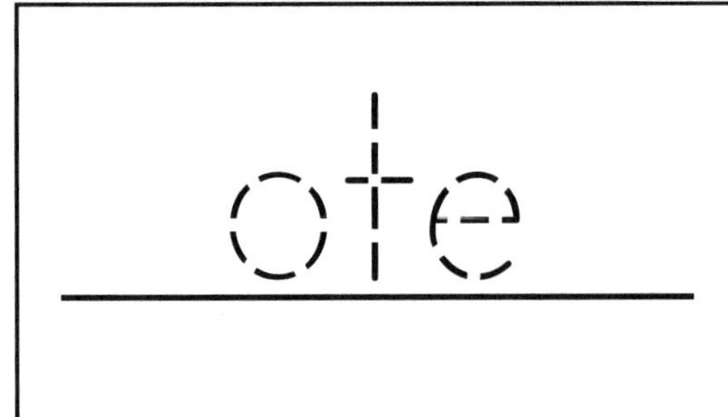

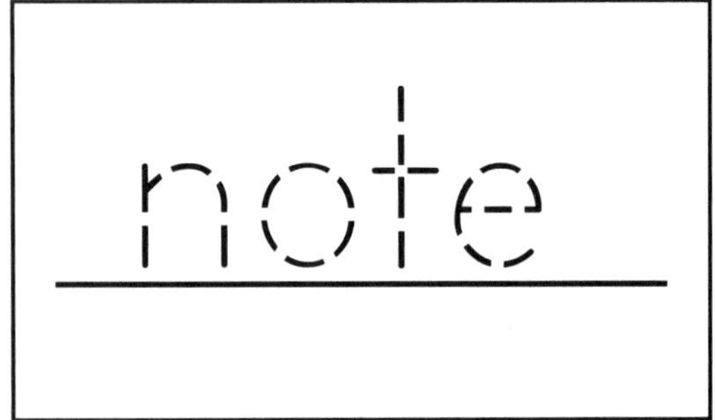

Here is a ____________________ for you, Mom.

Name ____________________

Dictated Phrases *note* and *vote*

1. ____

____

2. ____

____

3. ____

____

Name ____________________

Create *cone*

one

____

____

cone

____

____

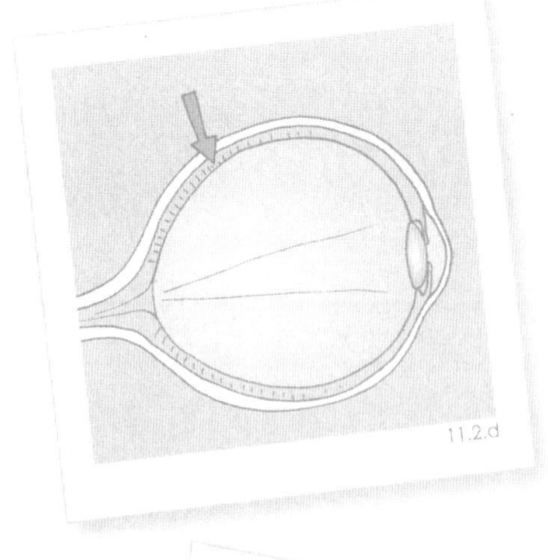

Bill walks by a ____________________.

Name ____________________

Dictated Phrases *cone* and *bone*

1. ______________________________________

____

2. ______________________________________

____

3. ______________________________________

____

Name ______________________

Create *cube*

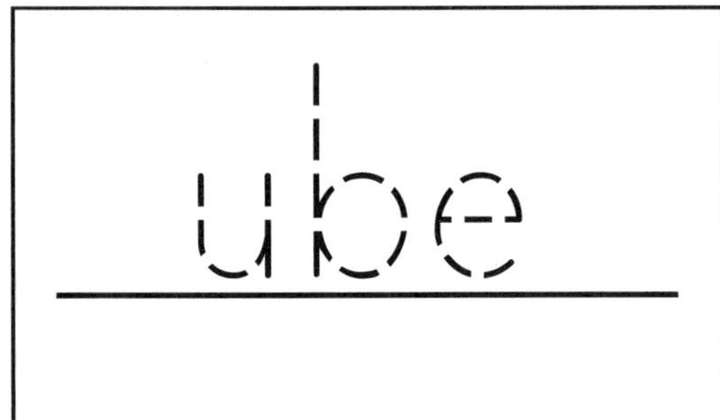

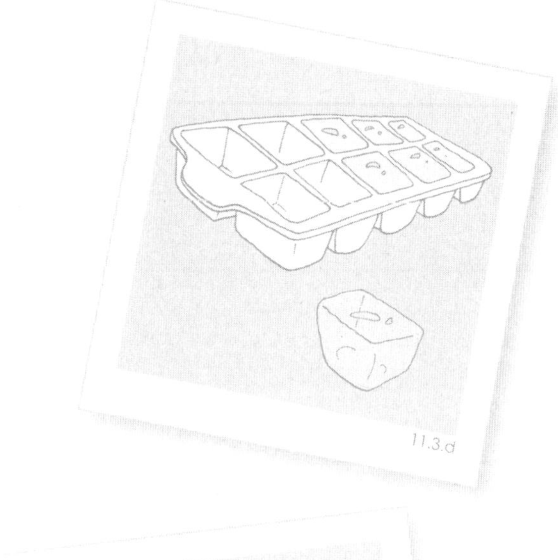

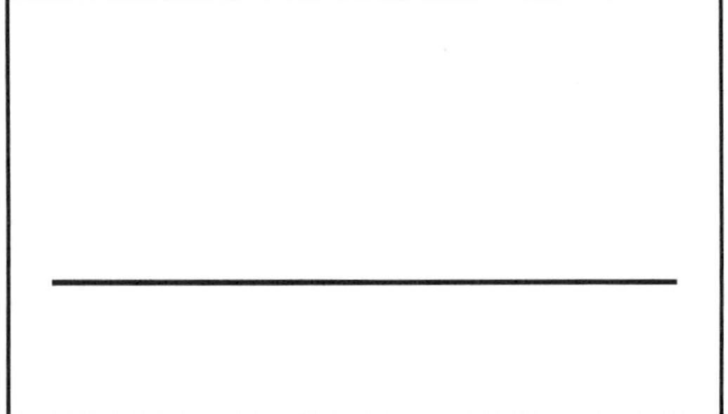

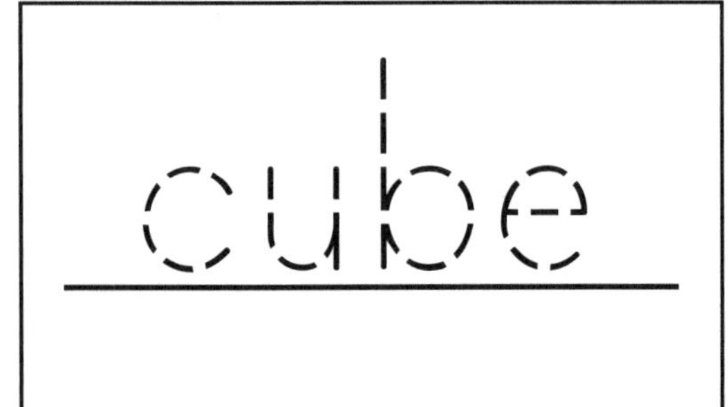

Put an ice ______________ in the glass.

Name ______________________

Create *tube*

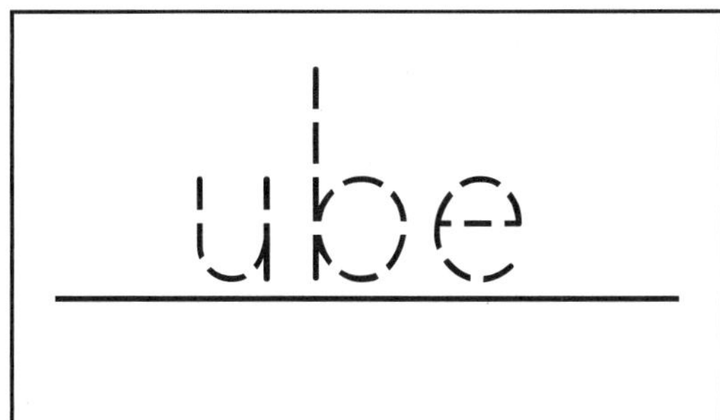

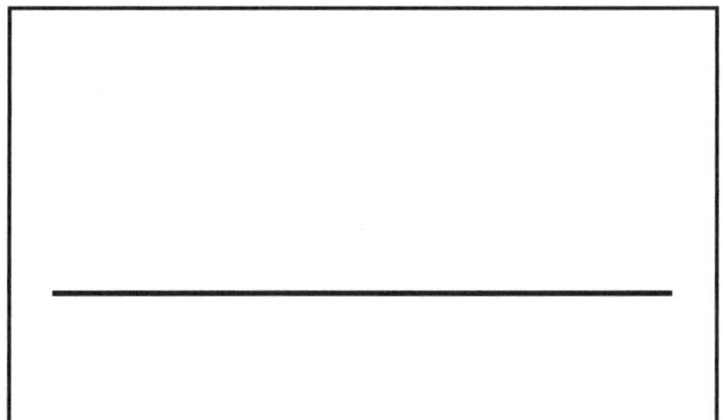

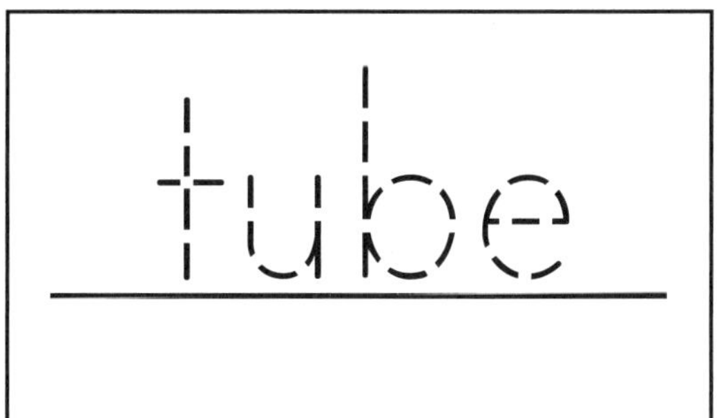

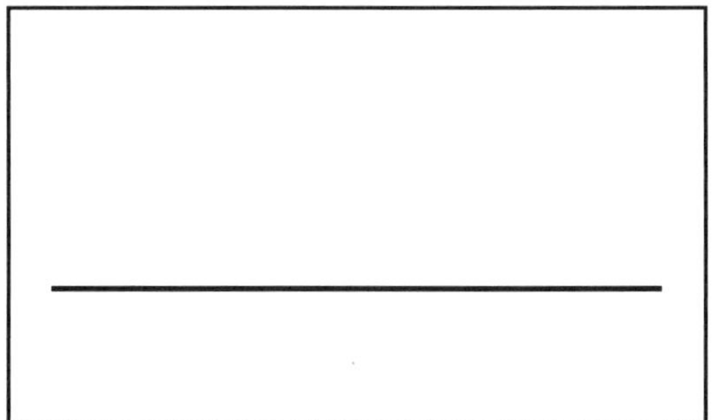

Bob taps the test ______________.

Name ____________________

Dictated Phrases *cube* and *tube*

1. ____

____

2. ____

____

3. ____

____

Name ______________________

Eye-Spy Words

Units 2–9

the	do	I	get	that	when	as
is	on	are	from	me	why	them
in	not	of	what	out	where	go
a	see	he	my	but	who	they
this	at	by	was	so	how	here
and	it	with	little	Mom	very	there
has	she	for	him	then	water	
	his	to	we	up	says	
	happy	said	if		you	
					no	

Units 10–11

wants
have
her
make
like
all
off
were

____

____

____

____

____

Name ______________________

"The Cape Cod Fishing Date"

"Do you want to go to Cape Cod to fish?" says Pop.
Bill and Bob dig fishing!
"I can get a fish for dinner," says Bill.

They ride to Cape Cod with Pop.
Bill gets on a big rock to fish.

The rock rocks!
Bob says, "The rock will tip!"
Pop says, "Bill, you will fall!"

Just then a fish bites Bill's line.
Bit by bit, Bill tugs on his line.
He has a big fat catfish!
What a fisherman!

But the fish pines for the water.
The fish outwits Bill. He tips his fin and escapes.

"No fish for dinner!" yells Bob.

"We are in luck," says Pop with a wink, and digs for his bag by the rocks.

In a wink, they dine on ham and a bag of dates.
"That was a fine dinner date," they all said.

Time taken:

2nd reading ____________ 2nd reading ____________ 3rd reading ____________

Name ______________________

Making Words With Magic-*e*

Real Words	Non-Words

UNIT 11

Name ___________________

Create *use*

use
____

____

use
____

____

Which pen can I _______________?

Name ____________________________

Dictated Phrases *use* and *muse*

1. ____

____

2. ____

____

3. ____

____

Name ____________________

RAN Chart (Core Words)

note	cone	cube	use
tube	use	cone	note
use	cone	cube	tube

Time taken:

2nd reading ____________ 2nd reading ____________ 3rd reading ____________

Name ______________________

RAN Chart (Core Words + Review)

date	cone	cane	use
fine	cape	pine	note
use	cone	cube	tube

Time taken:

2nd reading ____________ 2nd reading ____________ 3rd reading ____________

Name ____________________

Writing Sentences for Image Cards

Select the appropriate sentence from the bottom of the page to describe the picture. Write the sentence on the lines underneath the picture.

11.3.b

____

____

11.2.b

____

____

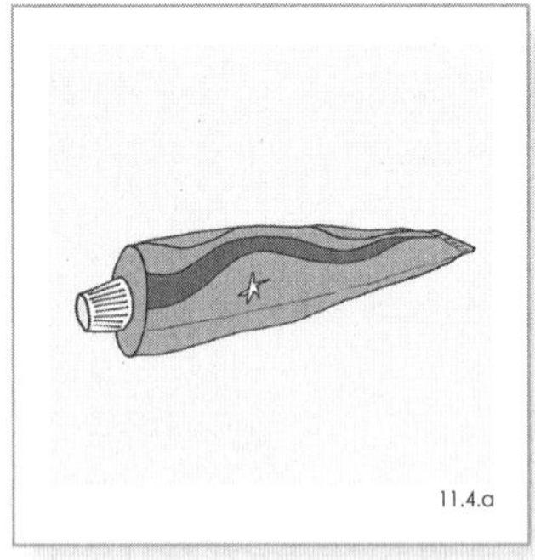
11.4.a

____

____

11.1.d

____

____

I have notes in my bag.

I cut the cube.

The cone is in the lane.

I can use a tube.

Name ____________________

Rime Family Words

ane	ape	ate	ine	ote	one	ube	use
cane	cape	date	fine	note	cone	cube	use
lane	tape	gate	line	rote	bone	tube	muse
mane	gape	late	mine	vote	lone	lube	
pane	grape	Kate	nine		tone		
sane		fate	pine		zone		
		mate			hone		

Name ___________________

"Zapcat and the Ticking Pinecone"

"You are a fine cat, Zapcat. You got my van out of the grape jam," said the man in the van.

Zapcat said, "Oh, I see it is going on nine. I must go to my date."

But just then, Zapcat saw a big pinecone in the pines with a note on it.

Zapcat tugged at the note. It said, "This cube is set to go off at nine!" The cube was ticking. "Tick ... tick ... "

"What?" said Zapcat. "This cannot go off! It will wake the cub and his mom. How can the man in the van escape?"

Zapcat used his Zap-hammer to tap the top of the cube and reset it for ten.

"My date will be happy we are out of that jam," said Zapcat.

The man in the van winked at Zapcat. "You can tell your date you made me a happy man!"

Time taken:

2nd reading ____________ 2nd reading ____________ 3rd reading ____________

Name ____________________

Ender Bender *s*

Write the words inside the ( ) on the blank lines and add Ender Bender ***s*** on them if they need it. Circle whether the word is used as a noun or a verb in the sentence.

1. Bob ____________ his ____________.
(ride) ***noun*** or ***verb***
(bike) ***noun*** or ***verb***

2. A fish ____________ Bill's line.
(bite) ***noun*** or ***verb***

3. The fish ____________ for the water.
(pine) ***noun*** or ***verb***

4. Sam ____________ a ____________ for his mom.
(make) ***noun*** or ***verb***
(note) ***noun*** or ***verb***

5. ____________ will fall out of the ____________.
(cone) ***noun*** or ***verb***
(pine) ***noun*** or ***verb***

Name ______________________

Rime Family Words

Real Words	Non-Words

UNIT 12

Name ______________________

Create *flat*

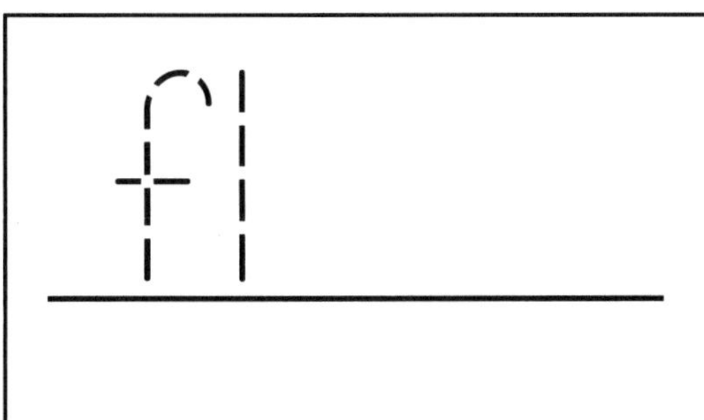

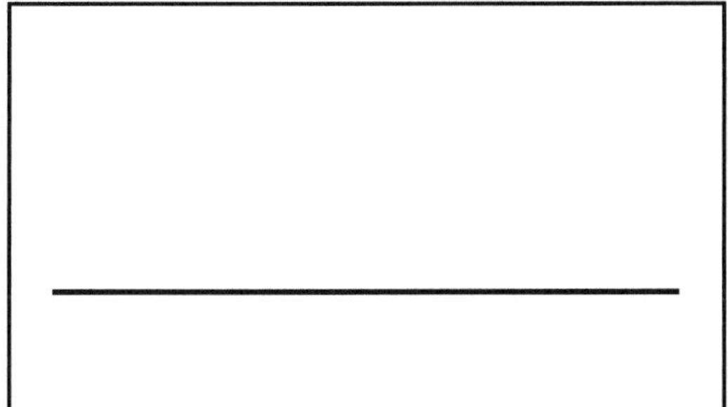

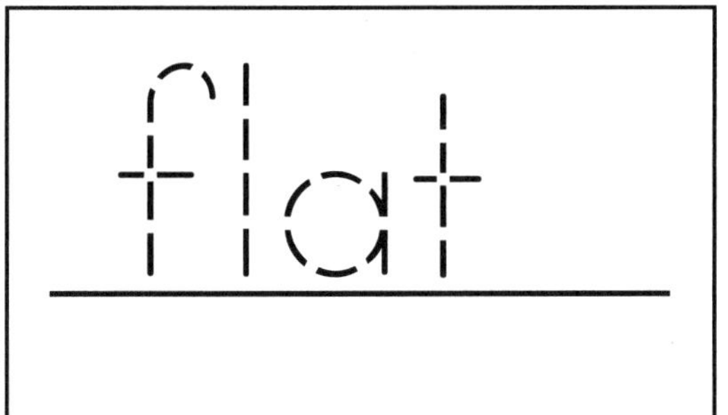

Yuck! This pop is ______________!

Name ______________________

Dictated Phrases *flat* and *flip*

1. ____

____

2. ____

____

3. ____

____

Name ______________________

Create *plan*

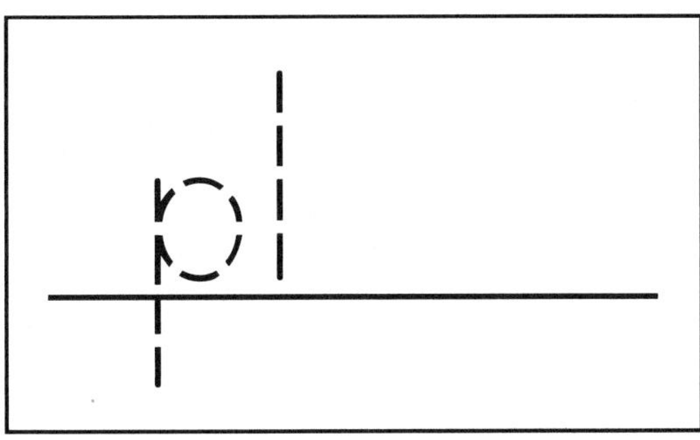

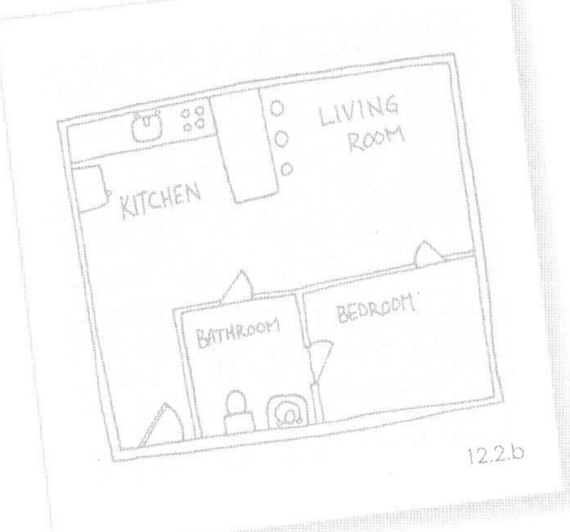

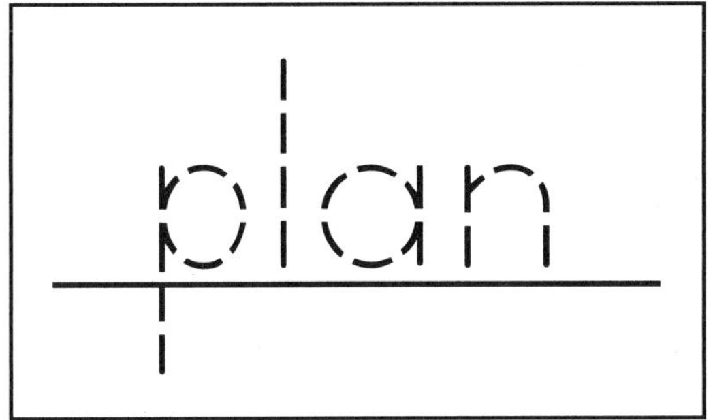

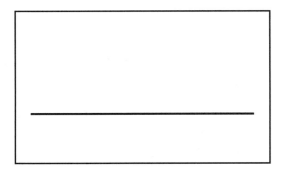

She has a ______________ to win the game.

Name ____________________

Dictated Sentences *plan* and *plug*

1. ____

____

2. ____

____

3. ____

____

Name ____________________

Harder Starter Words (*fl* and *pl*)

Highlight Harder Starters and Ender Benders first. Make sure to highlight only the starter, not the whole word. Read first for accuracy and then for speed. Then check for comprehension.

fl words

The flat flip-flop flips and flaps in the sand.

They flap a flag as they flock to the game.

pl words

I can pluck the plug from the can.

I plan to plug in the plug if we can pluck it out.

fl and *pl* words

The flan is on the plate.

Plan to flap the flag.

The plan was a flop.

Name ______________________

Sound Sliders *fl*

Harder Starter: fl______________

Real Words	Non-Words

Name ______________________

Sound Sliders *pl*

Harder Starter: pl

Real Words	Non-Words

Name ____________________

Create *trap*

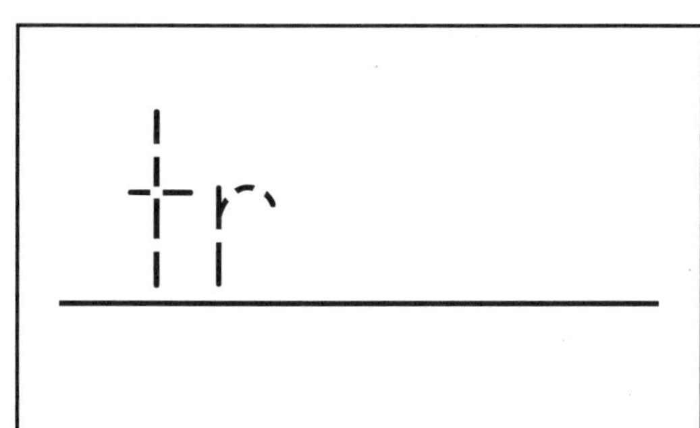

12.3.a

12.3.c

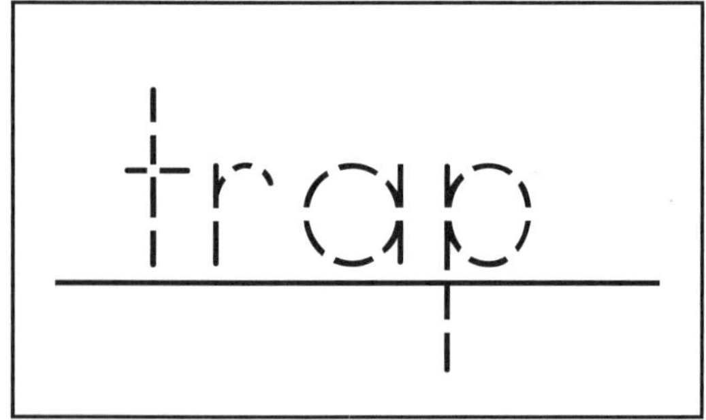

12.3.b

The rat is by the __________.

Name ______________________

Dictated Phrases *trap* and *trip*

1. ____

____

2. ____

____

3. ____

____

Name ______________________

Create *track*

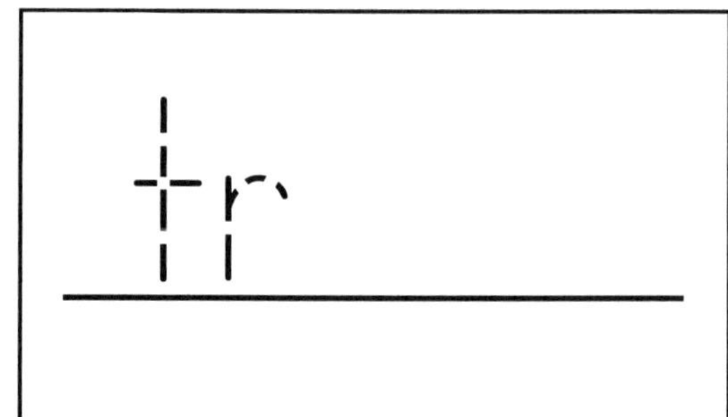

12.4.a

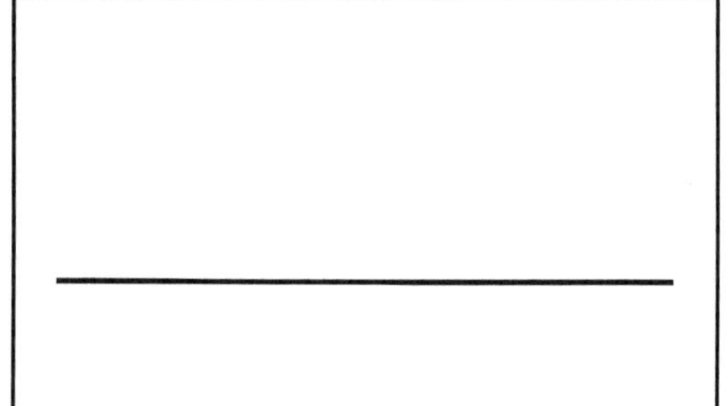

12.4.c

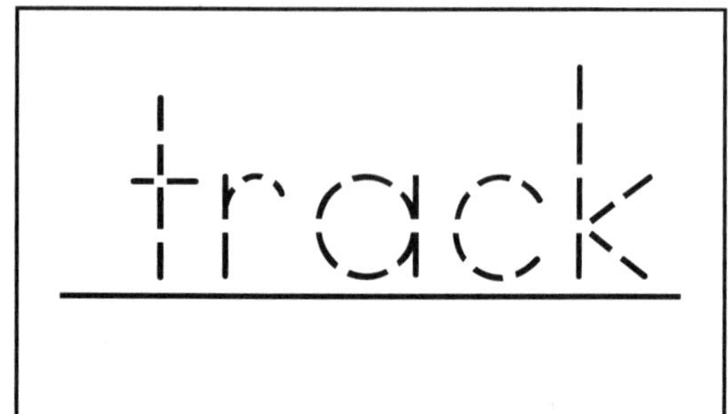

12.4.e

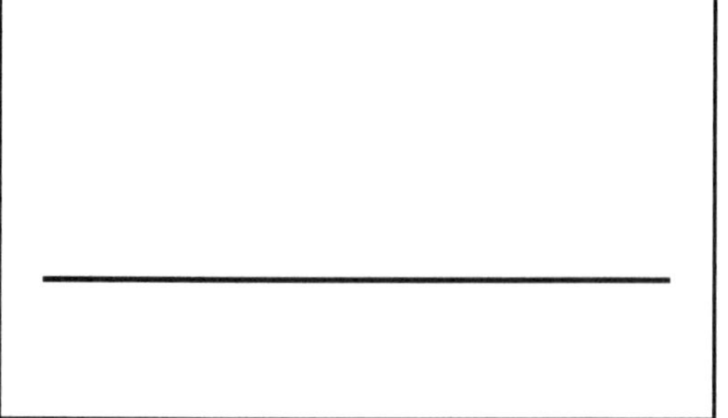

Jack runs on the ______________.

Name ____________________

Dictated Phrases *track* and *back*

1. ______________________________

____

2. ______________________________

____

3. ______________________________

____

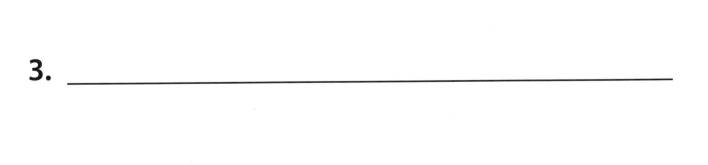

Name ______________________

Write and Compare Words

ick	*ack*

uck	*ock*

1. ______________________________

____

2. ______________________________

____

3. ______________________________

____

Name ____________________

Create *crab*

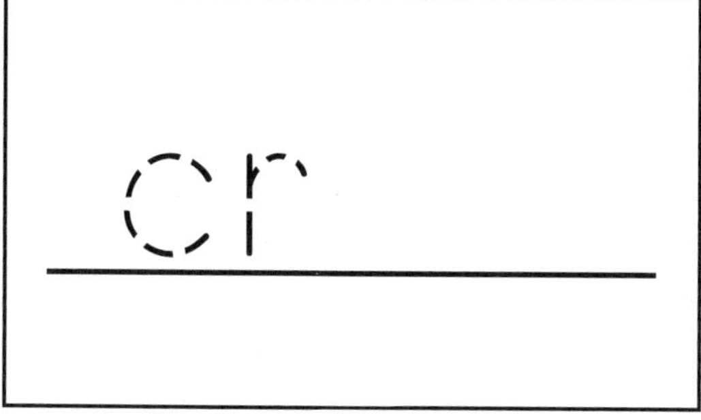

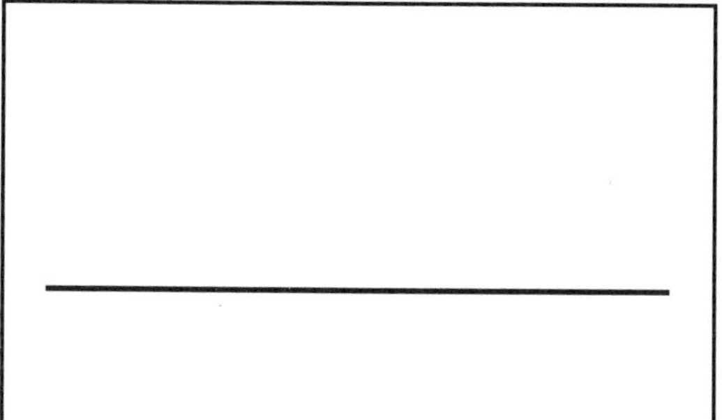

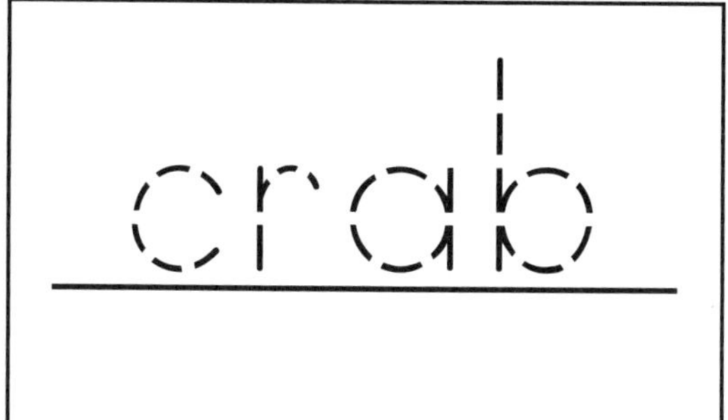

The ____________ is in the sand.

Name ____________________

Dictated Sentences *crab, crop,* and *lab*

1. ____

____

2. ____

____

3. ____

____

Name ____________________

Eye-Spy Words

Units 2–9

the
is
in
a
this
and
has

do
on
not
see
at
it
she
his
happy

I
are
of
he
by
with
for
to
said

get
from
what
my
was
little
him
we
if

that
me
out
but
so
Mom
then
up

when
why
where
who
how
very
water
says
you
no

as
them
go
they
here
there

Units 10–12

wants
have
her
make
like
all
off
were
wink
your

saw

Name ______________________________

"Tracking the Tracks by the Tracks"

Sam is a tracker.
Sam has a big mystery.

He sees tracks.
He sees tracks by the rocks.

He sees tracks in the sand.
He sees tracks by the tracks!

"What is this?" said Sam.
"I must plan to track it."

"The tracks are flat and not so big, so it must not be big.
Tracking it will be fun. Then I will trap it."

Sam is in the sand. He has it!
What did Sam track and trap?
(Hint: See the tracks!)

Yes, you got it!
The madcap duck!

Time taken:

2nd reading ____________ 2nd reading ____________ 3rd reading ____________

Name ______________________

Harder Starter *tr*

Harder Starter: ______________

Real Words

Name ____________________

Rime Family *ack*

Rime Family: ______________

Real Words

Name ______________________

Create *stand*

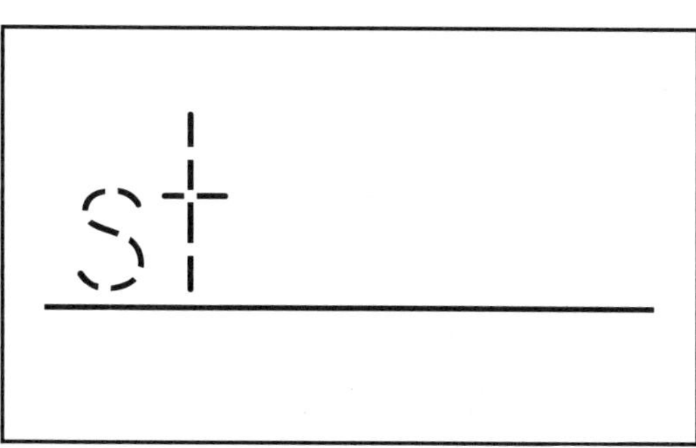

12.6.a

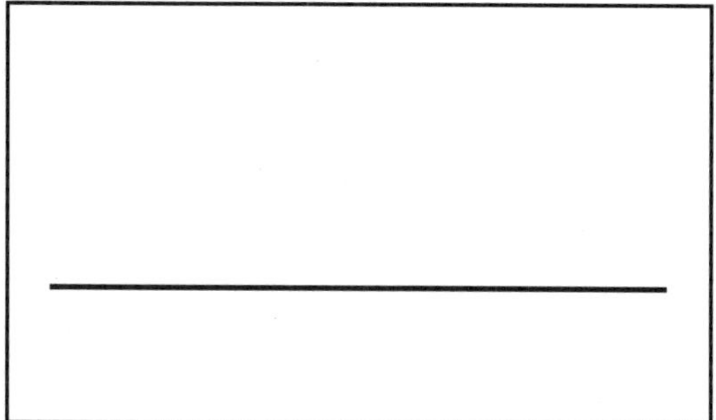

12.6.b

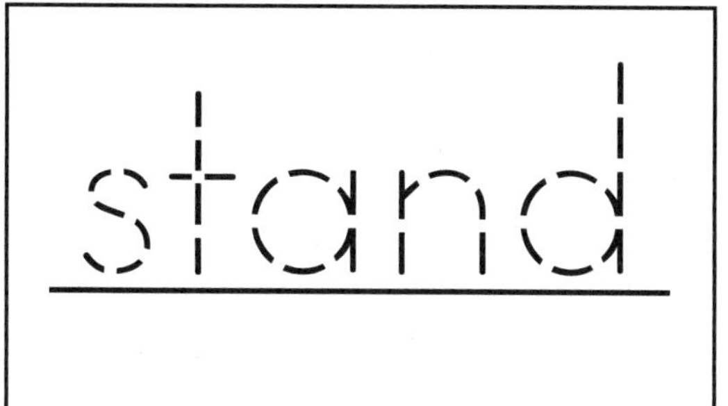

12.6.c

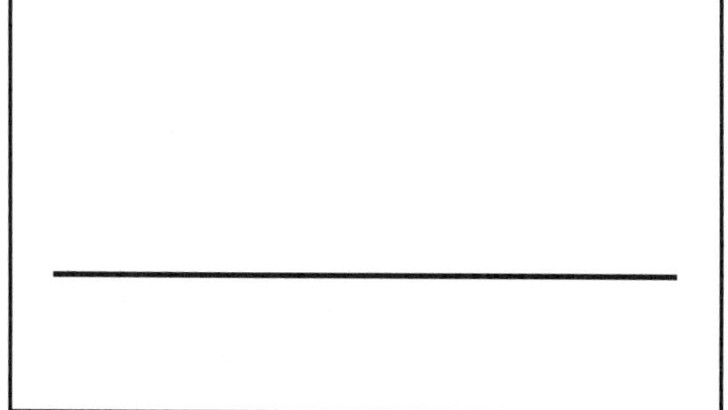

______________ by the track.

Name ___________________________

Dictated Sentences ***stand*, *stop*, and *band***

1. ____

____

2. ____

____

3. ____

____

Name ______________________

"Jack on the Track"

This is Jack. Jack likes running.

Jack wants to run on the track and win.

The track is sand and has lines on it.

Jack has a plan for the flat track.

He will run flat out and win!

Jack stands at the back. He can see his fans in the stands.

Crack! The runners go.
"Go Jack!" say the fans. Jack runs for home with the pack, but he is still at the back.

Rats! Jack is trapped in the jam-packed pack. He cannot escape the pack!
He cannot see the winning runner. But he can see his sad fans in the stands.

Jack says to his fans, "Winning is fine, but running is the best fun."

Time taken:

2nd reading ____________ 2nd reading ____________ 3rd reading ____________

Name ______________________

RAN Chart (Core Words)

trap	track	flat	plan
stand	crab	track	stand
trap	flat	crab	track

Time taken:

2nd reading ____________ 2nd reading ____________ 3rd reading ____________

Name ____________________

RAN Chart (Core Words + Review)

cape	plan	track	cone
trap	crab	tube	stand
fine	date	stand	flat

Time taken:

2nd reading ____________ 2nd reading ____________ 3rd reading ____________

Name ____________________

Ender Bender Worksheet

Core Word	*s*	*ing*	*ed*	*er*
trap	traps			
track			tracked	
flat		×	×	
plan			planned	
stand		standing	×	×
crab	crabs			

Name ______________________

"Runes in the Dunes"

Jane and Mike go for a hike.
In the sand dunes, they find a lone stone.

Mike sees the top of the stone is flat and has lines on it.
Jane says, "There are runes on the stone! Do not step on it."

"What are runes?" says Mike.
"Back in time, men did not have notepads so they made lines on rocks," Jane says.

Jane and Mike track the lines.

The lines are like cracks. "Runes are like magic plans," says Jane. Jane and Mike want to unlock what the runes say, but they cannot.

Jane has made lines like the runes in her notepad.

They sit in the sand and muse on the runes.
What the lines say is a mystery!

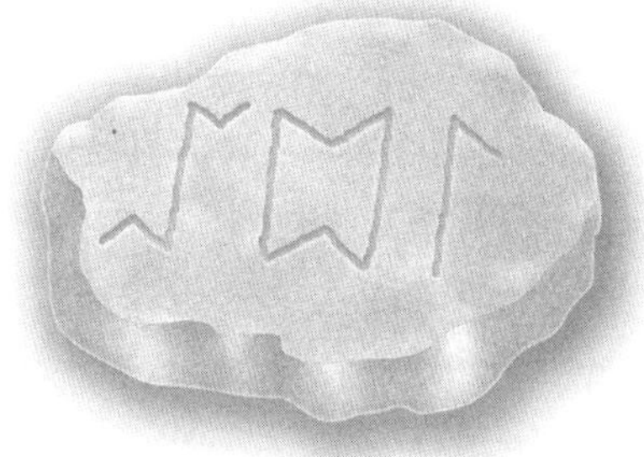

Time taken:

2nd reading __________ 2nd reading __________ 3rd reading __________

Name ______________________________

Word Creation

Real Words	Non-Words

Ticket Out the Door

1. ______________________________

2. ______________________________

3. ______________________________

4. ______________________________

5. ______________________________

6. ______________________________

Name ____________________

Create *trim*

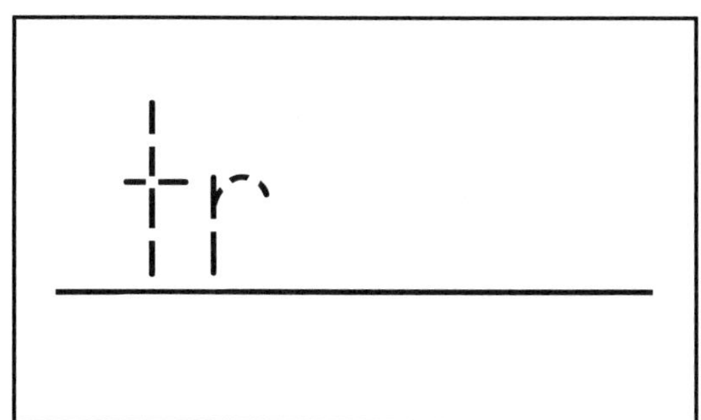

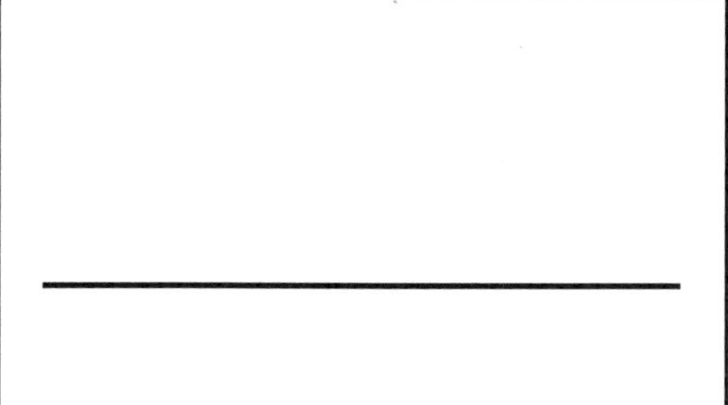

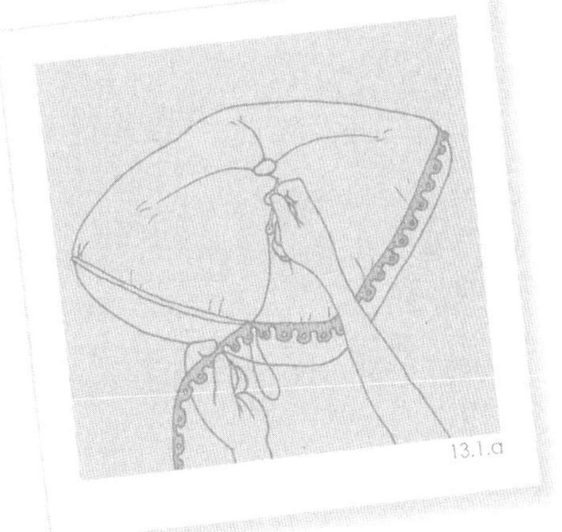

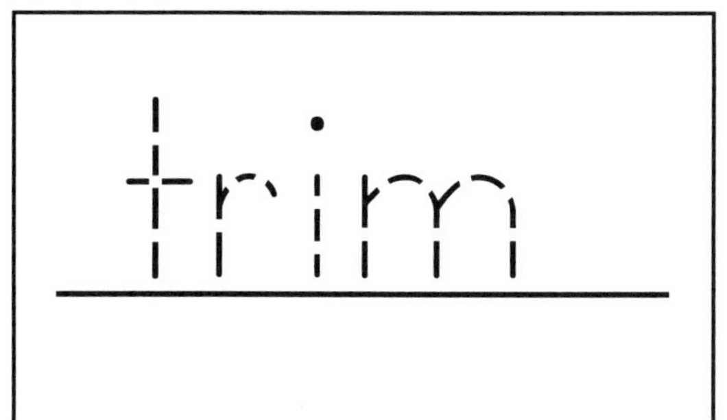

He will ______________ the dog with clippers.

Name ______________________________

Dictated Sentences *trim* and *rim*

1. ____

____

2. ____

____

3. ____

____

Name ______________________

Create *slip*

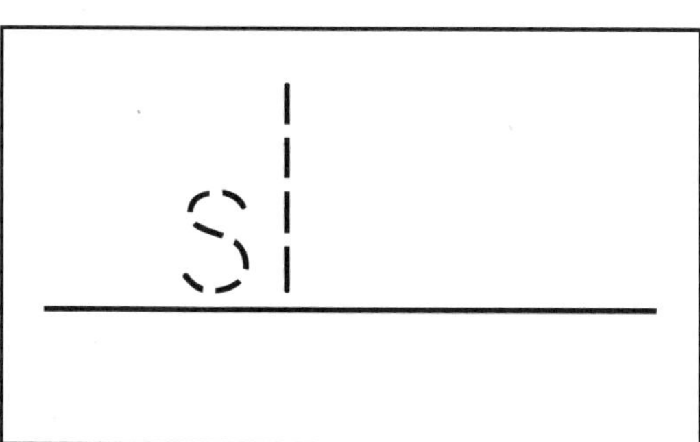

13.2.a

13.2.b

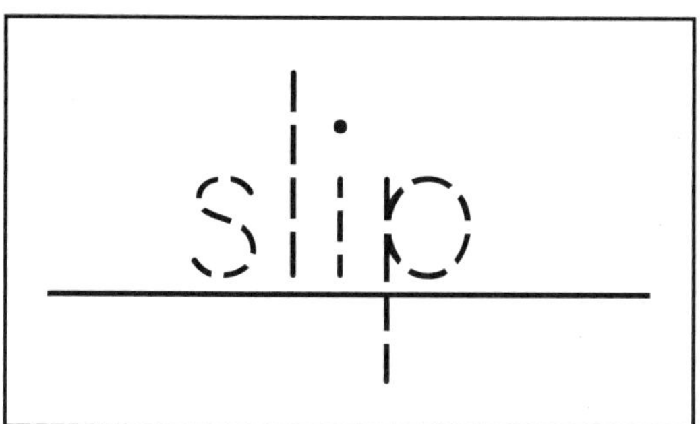

13.2.c

Pam and Bill __________ on the track.

Name ____________________

Dictated Phrases *slip* and *slick*

1. ____

____

2. ____

____

3. ____

____

Name ______________________

Dice Are Nice!

Real Words	Non-Words

Name ______________________

Create *ship*

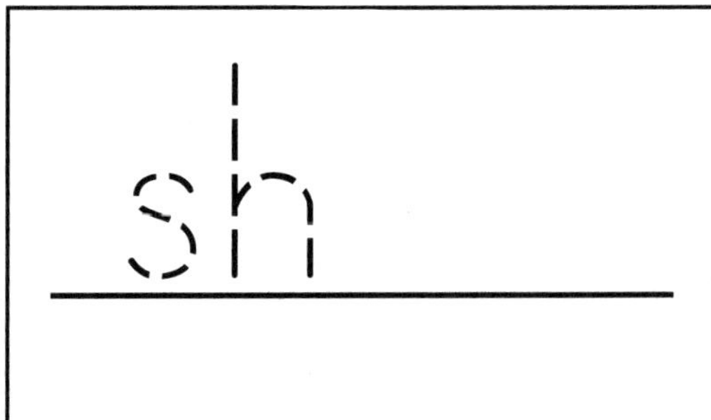

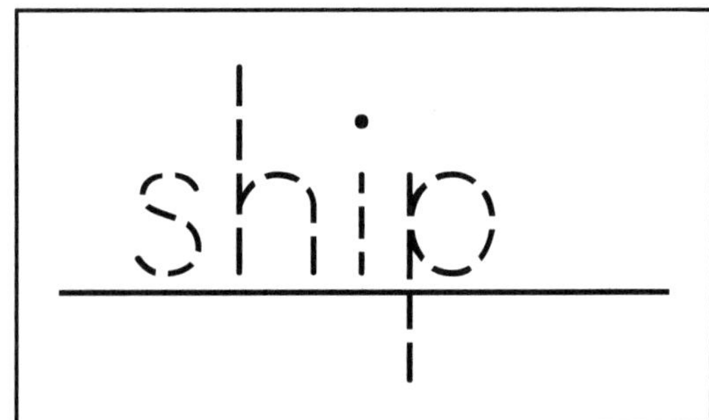

Chip and Jill ______________ a pack of nuts to Jack.

Name ______________________

Dictated Sentences *ship* and *shin*

1. ____

____

2. ____

____

3. ____

____

Name ______________________

Create *chip*

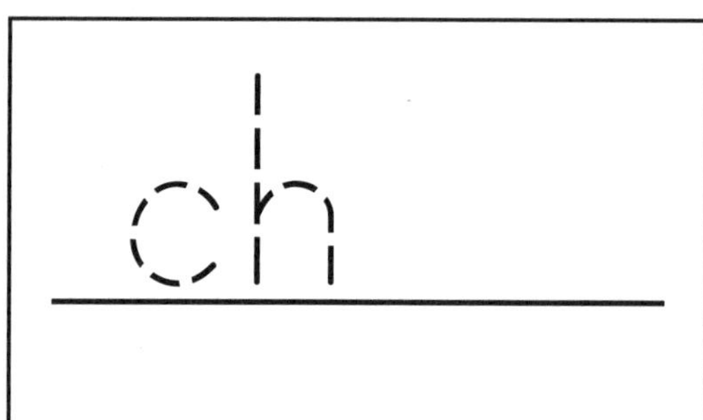

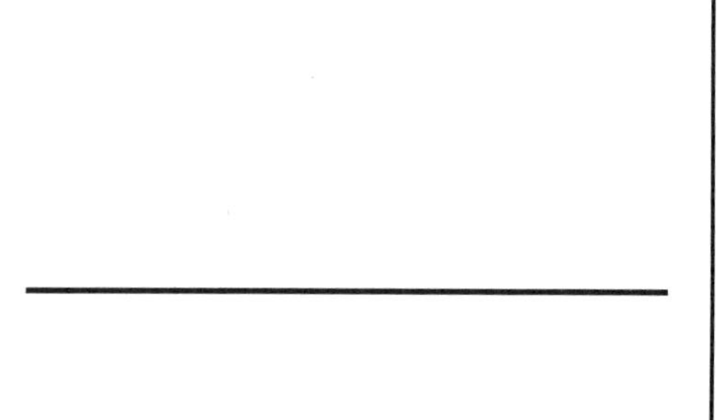

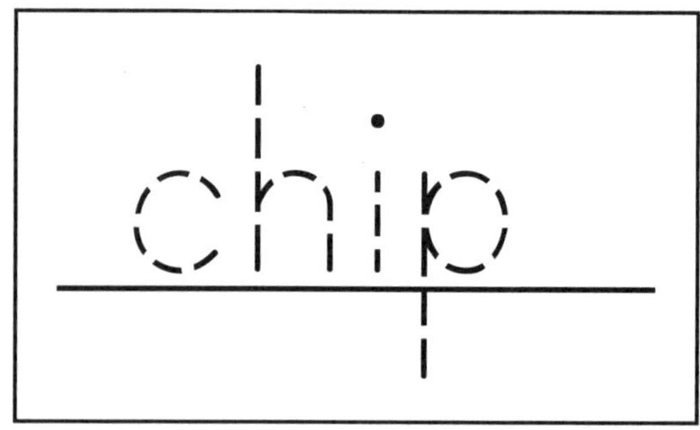

The dish has a ______________ in it.

Name ______________________

Dictated Phrases *chip* and *chill*

1. ______________________________

____

2. ______________________________

____

3. ______________________________

____

UNIT 13 Name ________________________

Ender Bender *y* Worksheet

1. It is a ________________ lane.
(sand)

2. The bike is ________________.
(rust)

3. Jack is ________________.
(crab)

4. The lake is ________________.
(chop)

5. My locker is ________________.
(dust)

6. That job is a bit ________________.
(trick)

7. My hat is ________________ and ________________.
(sag) (flop)

8. I am ________________ that she is ________________.
(luck) (wit)

Name ______________________

Write Words With Ender Bender *y*

1. ______________________

2. ______________________

3. ______________________

4. ______________________

5. ______________________

6. ______________________

7. ______________________

8. ______________________

Sentence 1. ______________________

____

Sentence 2. ______________________

____

Sentence 3. ______________________

____

Name ______________________

Create *spin*

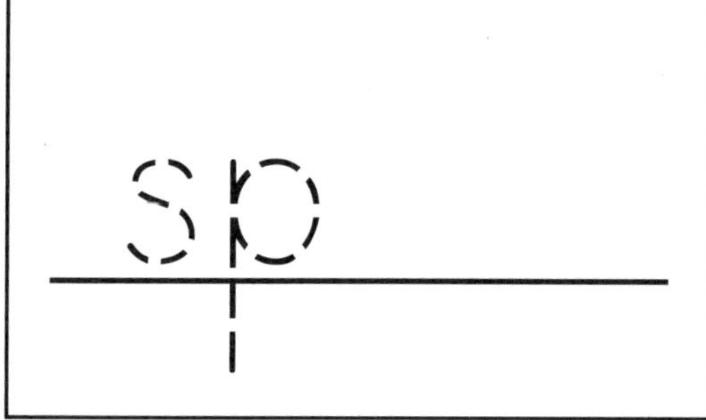

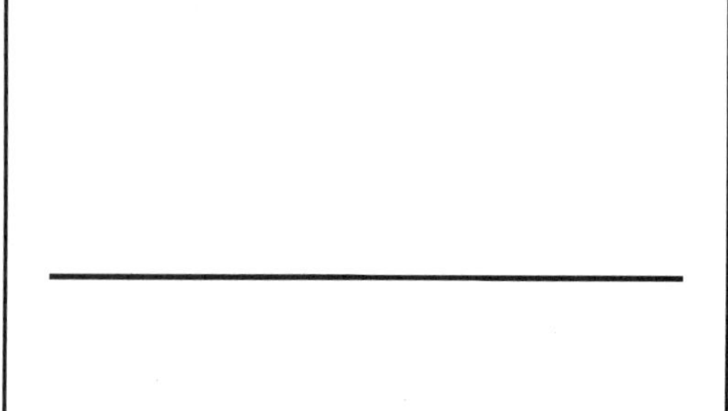

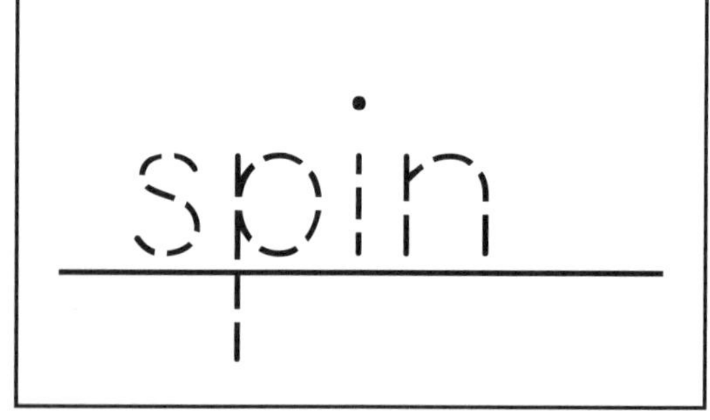

We can go out for a ______________.

UNIT 13

Name ______________________

Dictated Phrases *spin* and *spine*

1. ____

____

2. ____

____

3. ____

____

Name ____________________

Create *skip*

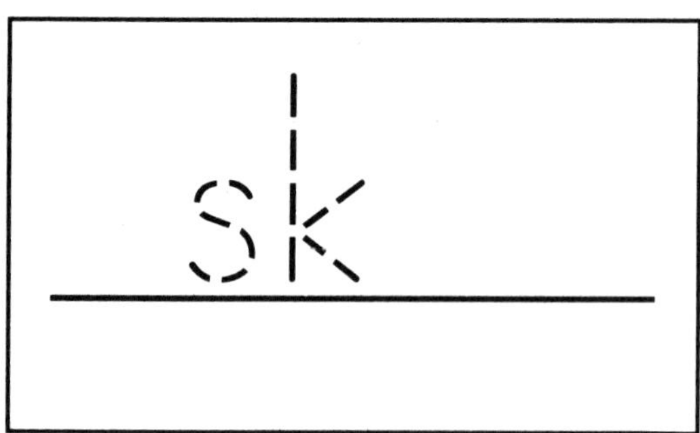

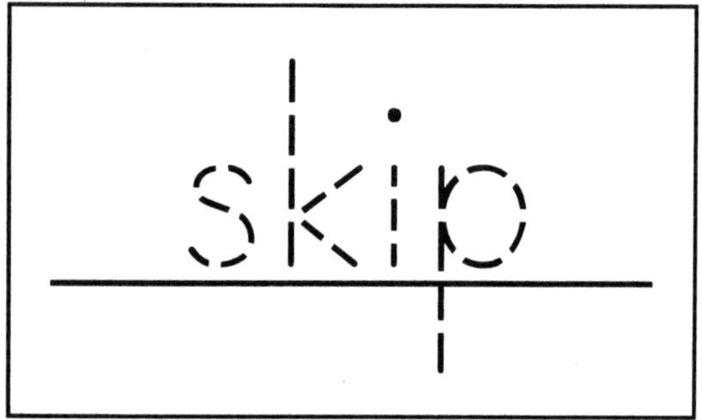

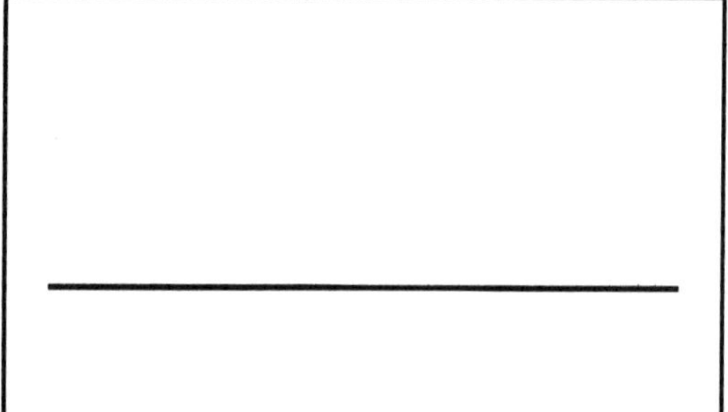

Did you ____________ a step?

Name ______________________

Dictated Sentences ***skip*** and ***skate***

1. ____

____

2. ____

____

3. ____

____

Name ____________________

"The Trip and the Ship"

Jim is tall, fit, and trim.
He likes to be by the lake.

Jim can run, flip, and spin. But there are times by the lake that he lacks a little fun.

"If I make a plan, I can still have fun," says Jim. "I can rig up a ship with a cape and a stick. It will go like a kite in the wind."

Jim trims the cape in a wink. He sticks it to the stick with sticky tape.

"I like this plan," says Jim. He runs and tugs the ship with the line. The ship bobs and rocks in the lake like the wind.

But oops! Jim trips and slips, and the ship tips and cracks.
The stick is chipped, and the cape is ripped.

Jim tracks back to the pines with no ship. What a sad trip!

Time taken:

2nd reading ____________ 2nd reading ____________ 3rd reading ____________

Name ______________________

Ticket Out the Door Word Lists

Harder Starters: ***st, tr, fl, cl, sh, ch***

Ender Benders: ***s, ing, er, ed, y***

______________________	______________________
______________________	______________________
______________________	______________________
______________________	______________________
______________________	______________________
______________________	______________________
______________________	______________________
______________________	______________________
______________________	______________________
______________________	______________________

Name ______________________________

Eye-Spy Words

Units 2–9

the	do	I	get	that	when	as
is	on	are	from	me	why	them
in	not	of	what	out	where	go
a	see	he	my	but	who	they
this	at	by	was	so	how	here
and	it	with	little	Mom	very	there
has	she	for	him	then	water	
	his	to	we	up	says	
	happy	said	if		you	
					no	

Units 10–13

wants	saw
have	yes
her	be
make	mystery
like	home
all	magic
off	
were	
wink	
your	

Name ______________________

"Mixed-Up Trish"

Mom said, "Trish, will you dig up the plants?"
But Trish got mixed up and dug up the ants!

Mom said, "Trish, trap the ants in a can."
But Trish got mixed up and put a can in the plants.

Mom said, "Trish, pick up ships for the kids."
But mixed-up Trish picked up kids with ships.

Mom said, "Trish, fill the cracks with sand."
But mixed-up Trish filled the slacks with sand.

Mom said, "Trish, stand the pots on the rack."
So Trish sanded the spots on the track.

Mom said, "Trish, just do what I wish!"
But Trish got mixed up and chipped a big dish!

Mom was going mad.
"Trish, stick to the plan!"
And Trish winked, "OK, Mom, I will pick up the stand."

Time taken:

2nd reading ____________ 2nd reading ____________ 3rd reading ____________

Name ______________________

RAN Chart (Core Words)

ship	slip	skip	spin
trim	chip	slip	spin
ship	trim	skip	chip

Time taken:

2nd reading ____________ 2nd reading ____________ 3rd reading ____________

Name ______________________

Harder Starters Worksheet

cr	*fl*

st	*pl*

tr	*ch*

Name ______________________________

Harder Starters Worksheet

sh	*sl*

sp	*sk*

Name ______________________

Writing Words

1.	
2.	
3.	
4.	
5.	
6.	
7.	
8.	
9.	
10.	
11.	

Name ______________________

"When the Cat Naps and the Pigs Jig"

Ram plans to jam with Duck, Bug, and Hen.
The Cat naps and will not jam.

Duck runs in with his fine cape.
Duck rocks and rocks.

Bug stands where he can see.
Bug trills a note.

Hen hops on the stand with her neck bob-bob-bobbing
to Ram's jamming.
As Ram jams, Duck ducks.
When Bug spins, Hen bobs.

Jack Pig jigs with his cane in his hand.
Then he hands Jill Pig a candy cane.

Jill has a fine time until she flips Cat with her cane.

Cat gets mad and rocks Hen off the stand,
Hen bugs Bug, Bug nips the Pigs, the Pigs ram Ram,
and the Duck ducks!

What a rocking, rocky time!

Time taken:

2nd reading ____________ 2nd reading ____________ 3rd reading ____________

Name ____________________

What's in the Picture?

1.		9.	
2.		10.	
3.		11.	
4.		12.	
5.		13.	
6.		14.	
7.		15.	
8.		16.	

Name ______________________

RAN Chart (Core Words + Review)

spin	slip	pine	trim
chip	use	trap	stand
ship	cone	skip	cape

Time taken:

2nd reading ____________ 2nd reading ____________ 3rd reading ____________

Name ____________________

Create Harder Starter Words

 __ __ap	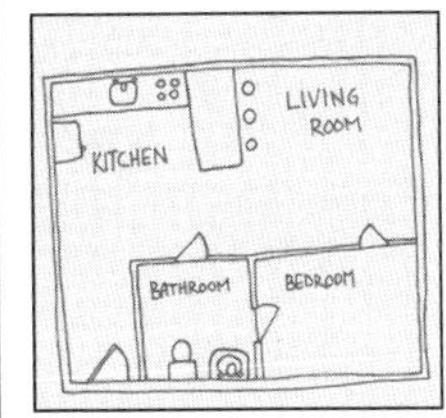 __ __an
 __ __ip	 __ __at
 __ __ab	 __ __ip
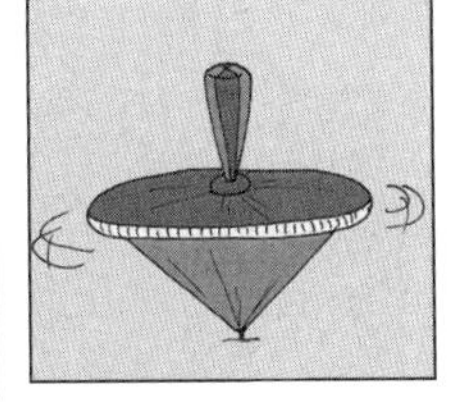 __ __in	 __ __ip
 __ __ip	 __ __ick

Name ________________

Create *grub*

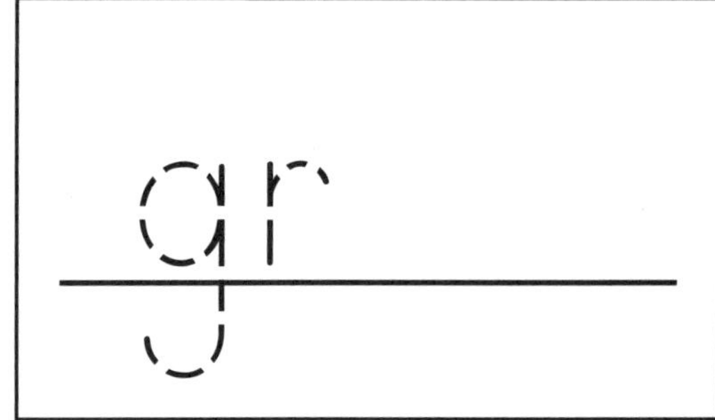

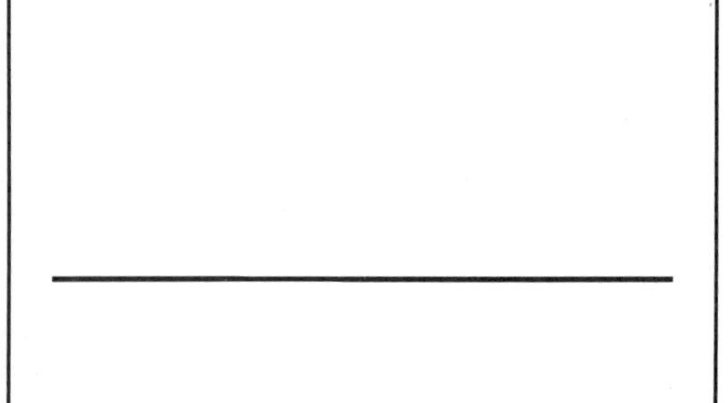

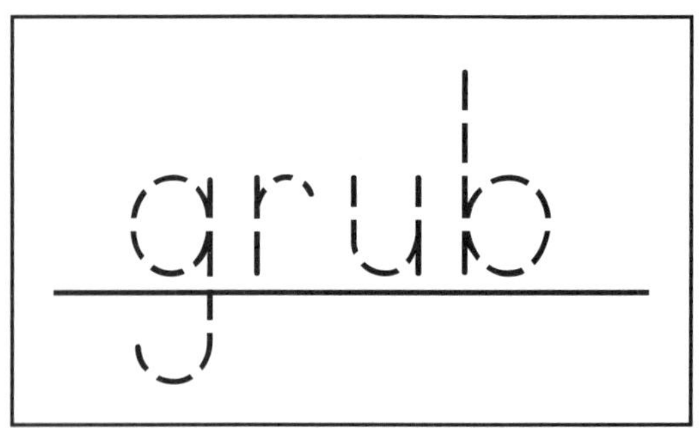

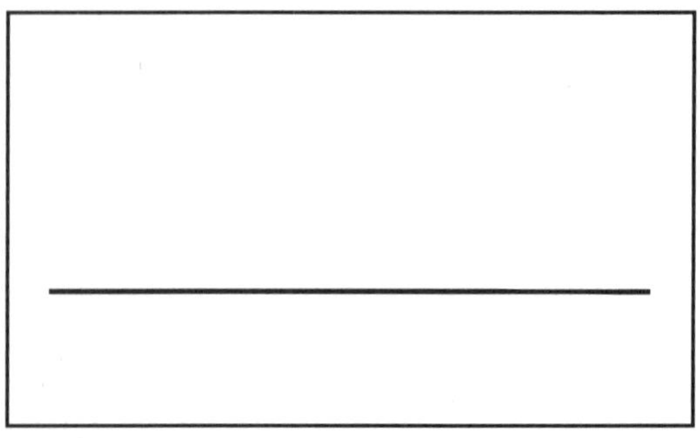

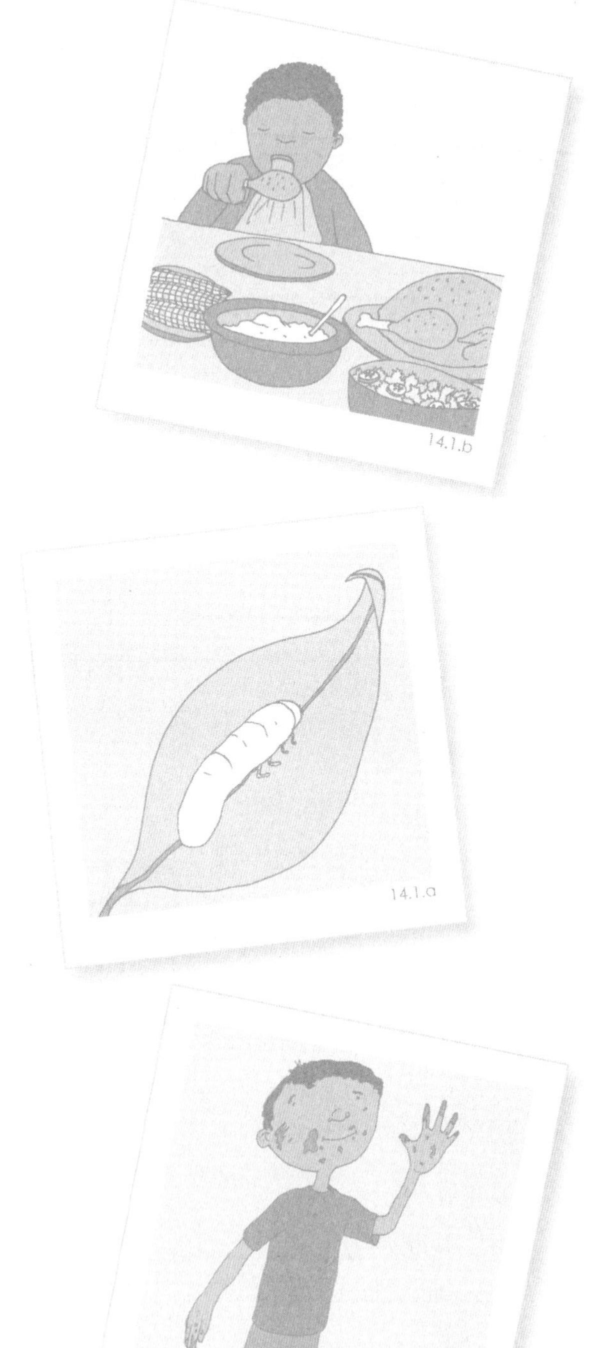

Let's plan to grab some ________________ after track.

Name ____________________

Dictated Sentences *grub* and *grill*

1. ____

____

2. ____

____

3. ____

____

Name ______________________

Create *brush*

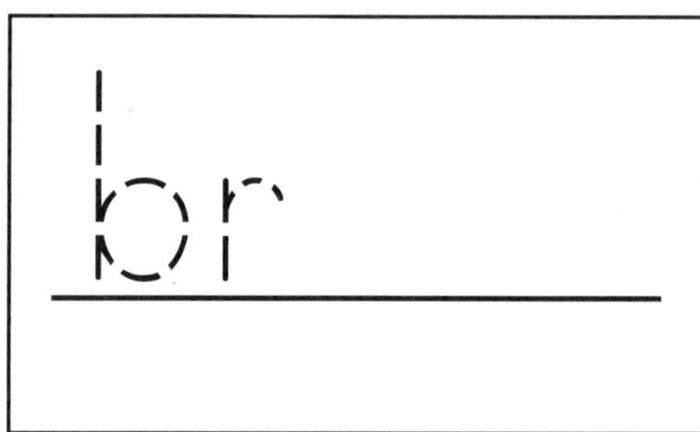

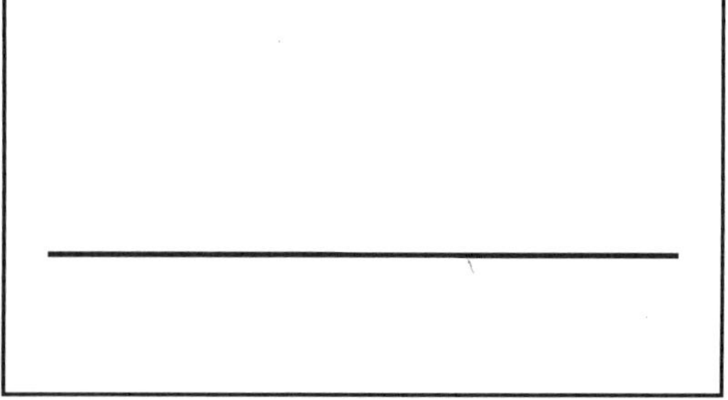

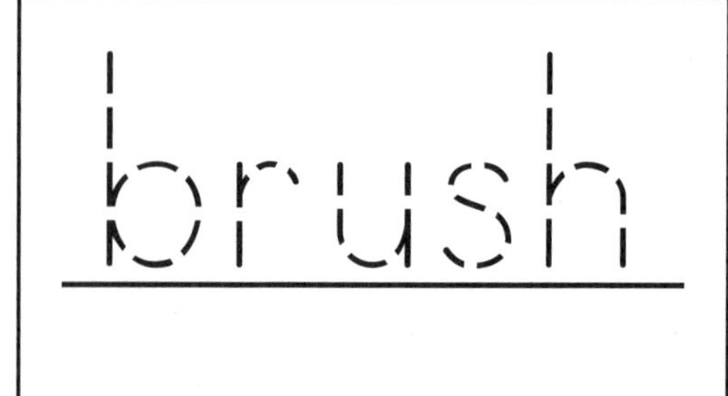

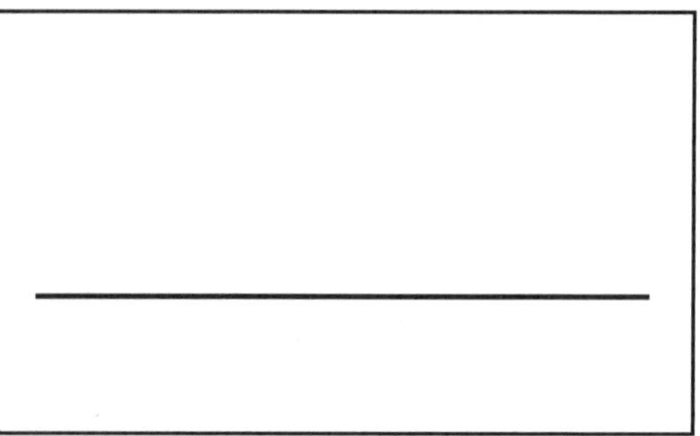

Do not ______________ me off!

Name ____________________

Dictated Sentences *brush*, *crush*, and *brand*

1. ____

____

2. ____

____

3. ____

____

Name ______________________

Make a Multitude of Words

Harder Starter: *gr*	Harder Starter: *br*

(continued)

Name ______________________

Make a Multitude of Words *(continued)*

Rime Pattern: ***ush***

1. ____

____

2. ____

____

3. ____

____

Name ____________________

Create *club*

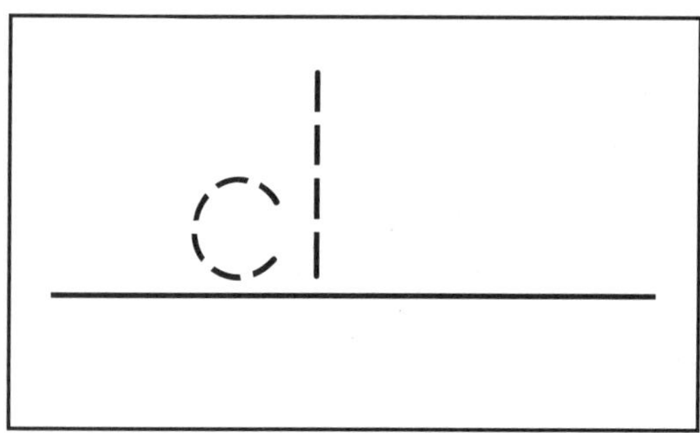

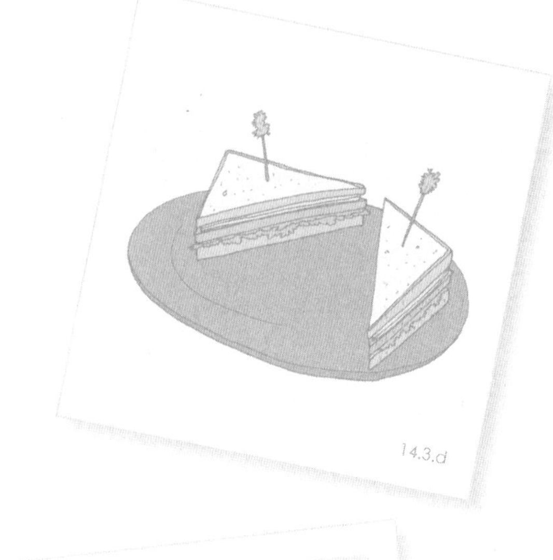

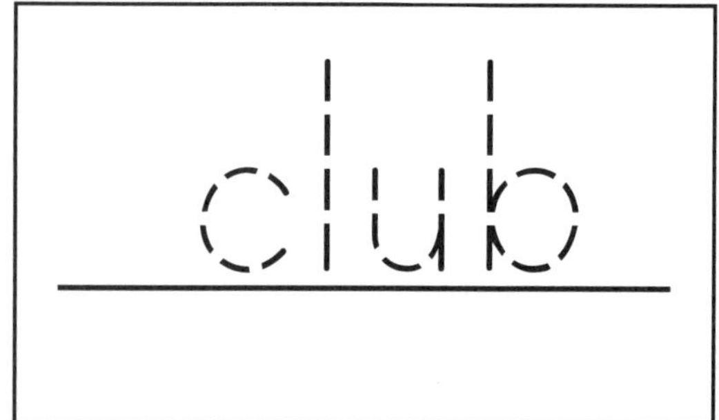

She had a ____________ sandwich for lunch.

Name ______________________________

Dictated Phrases *club* and *clip*

1. ____

____

2. ____

____

3. ____

____

Name ______________________

Create *slug*

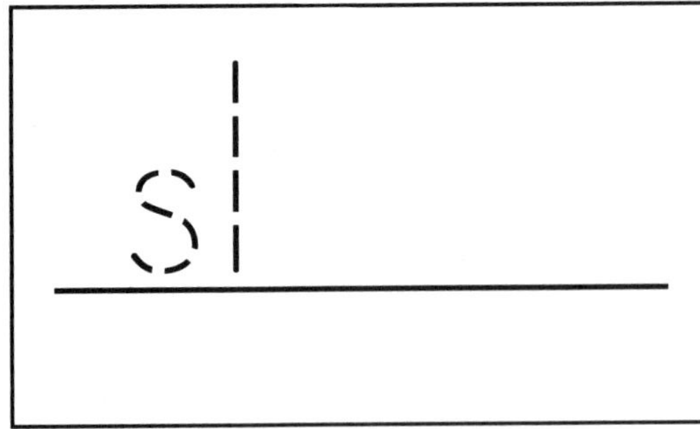

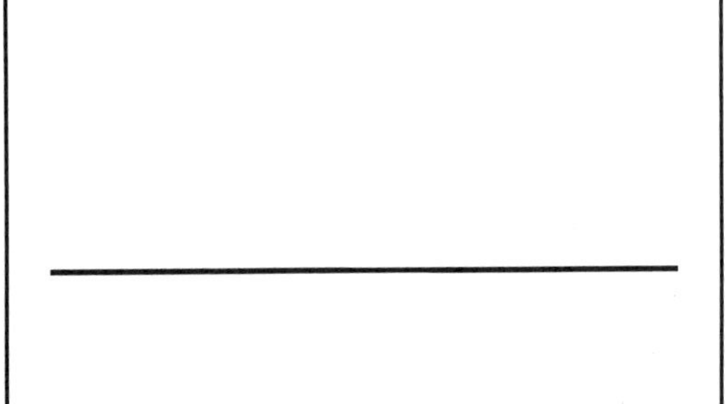

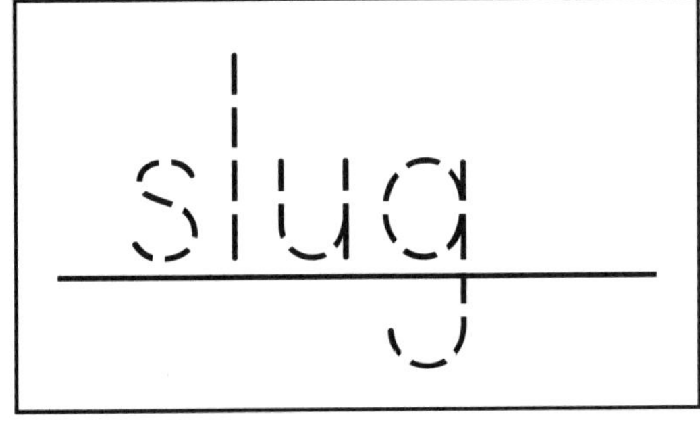

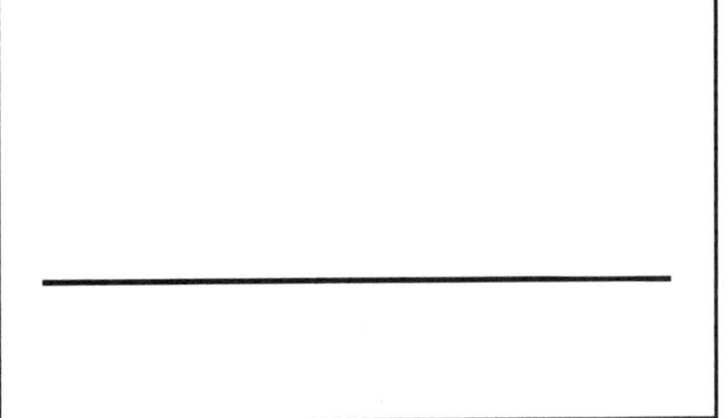

The ______________ and the bug are on the bed.

Name ______________________

Dictated Sentences *slug* and *slate*

1. ____

____

2. ____

____

3. ____

____

Name ______________________

Ender Bender *est*

flat

grim

thin

slim

hot

big

Name ____________________

Reading Word List

club	gram	bran	rush
clam	grill	brick	mush
click	grip	brine	gush
clip	grit	brand	crush
clock	grin	brim	flush
clot	grape	brag	plush
clone	grid	brad	lush
clack	grate	brig	hush

Time taken:

2nd reading ____________ 2nd reading ____________ 3rd reading ____________

UNIT 14 Name ______________________

Make Sentences Make Sense

Write the missing words in the spaces. Some words will have no Ender Bender, some will have ***er***, and some will have ***est***.

1. I am mad.

Bob is ______________.

Dan is the __________________.

2. My cat is ___________.

Jake's cat is sadder.

Bob's cat is the ________________.

3. I am _____________.

Mike is __________________.

Bill is the trimmest.

4. I can make a big flapjack, but Mom can make

a __________________ one.

5. I have a tall plant. Bob's is ________________,

but Kate has the ________________ one.

Name ______________________

Create *struck*

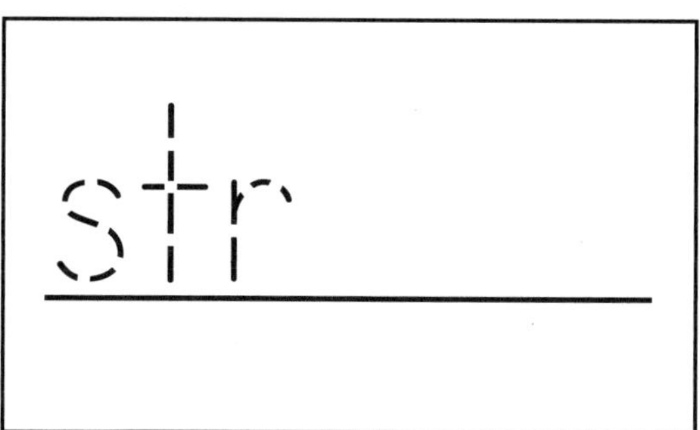

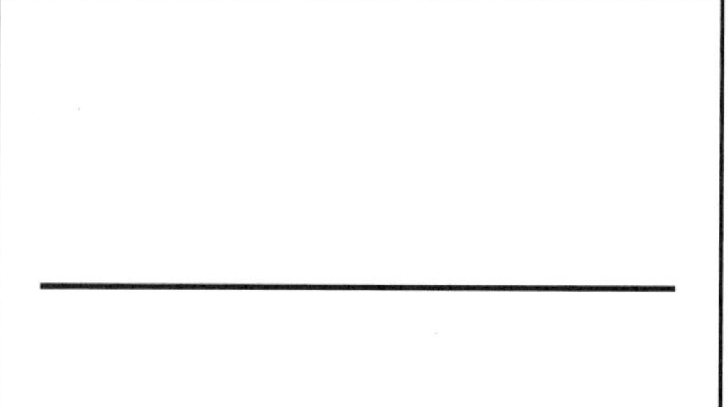

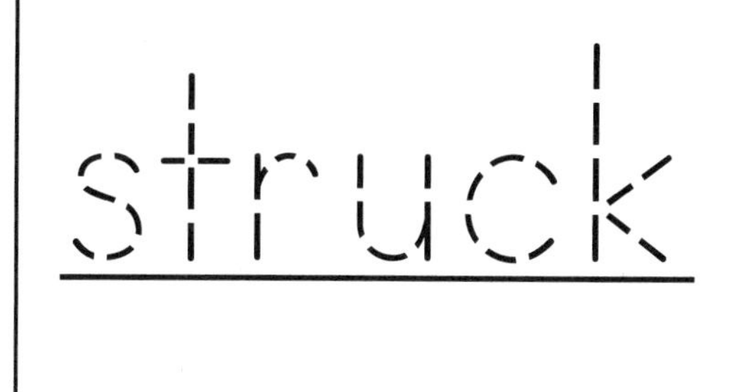

The kid ______________ out at bat.

Name ______________________

Dictated Sentences *struck* and *strip*

1. ____

____

2. ____

____

3. ____

____

UNIT 14

Name ______________________

Create *drum*

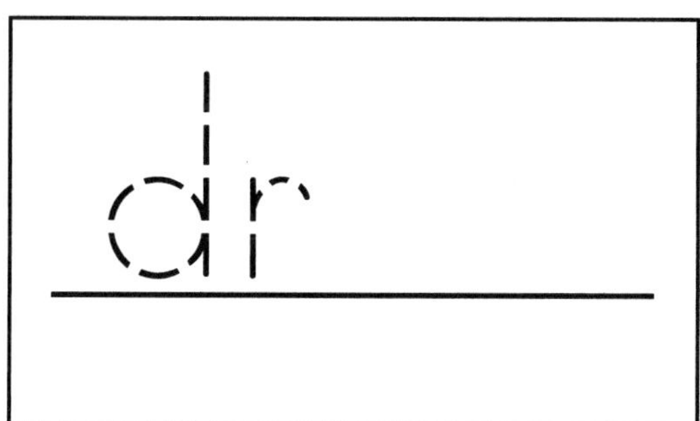

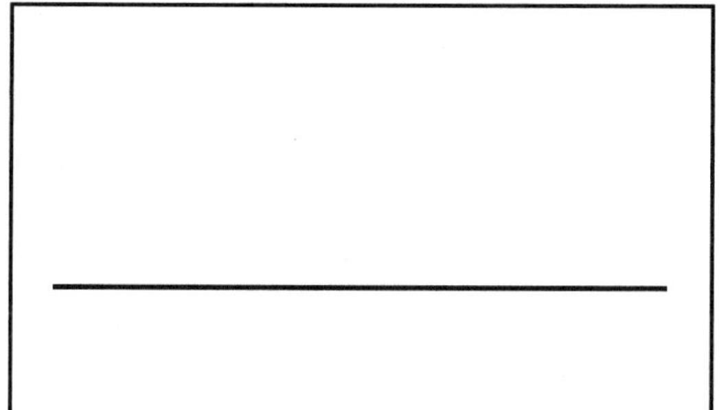

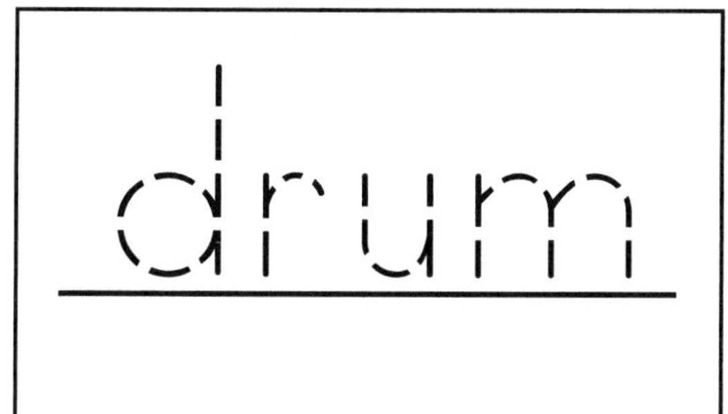

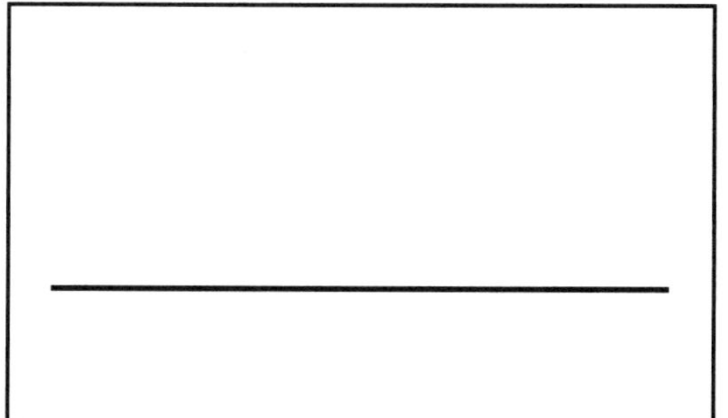

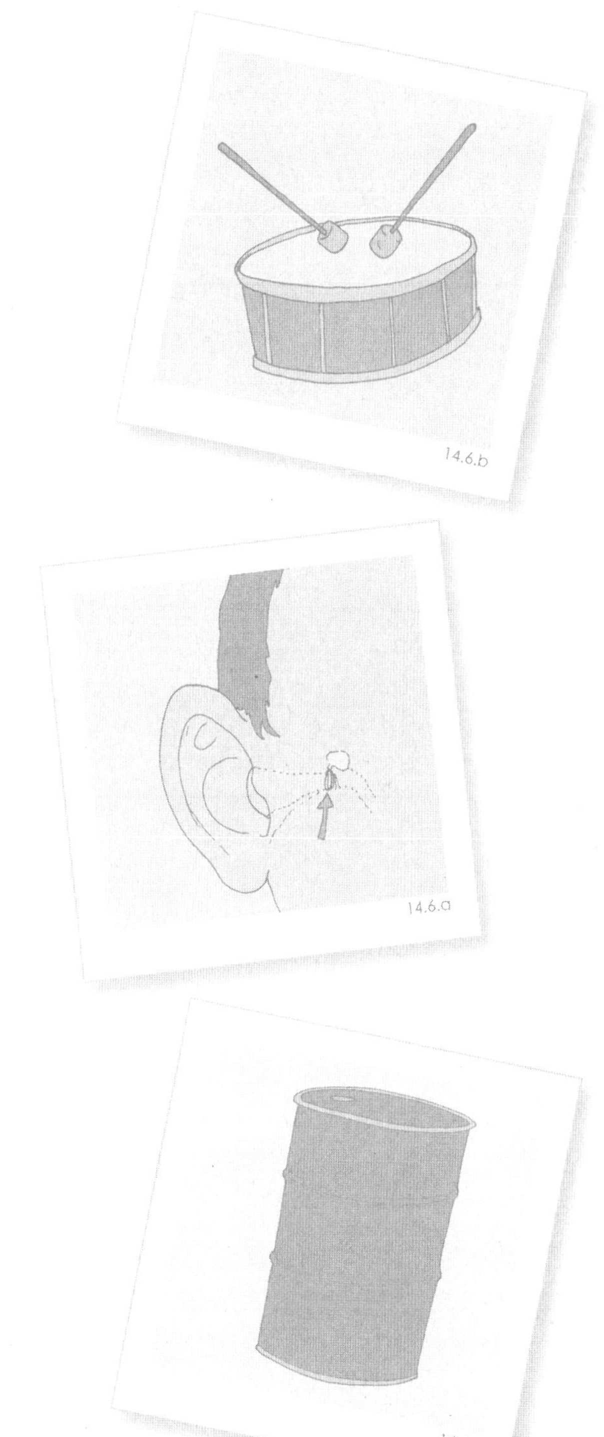

Stop hitting that ______________!

Name ______________________

Dictated Sentences *drum*, *gum*, and *drill*

1. ____

____

2. ____

____

3. ____

____

Name ______________________

Eye-Spy Words

Units 2–9

the
is
in
a
this
and
has

do
on
not
see
at
it
she
his
happy

I
are
of
he
by
with
for
to
said

get
from
what
my
was
little
him
we
if

that
me
out
but
so
Mom
then
up

when
why
where
who
how
very
water
says
you
no

as
them
go
they
here
there

Units 10–14

wants
have
her
make
like
all
off
were
wink
your

saw
yes
be
mystery
home
magic
put

____

____

____

____

____

Name ______________________

Dictated Phrases

1. ______________________________________

2. ______________________________________

3. ______________________________________

4. ______________________________________

5. ______________________________________

6. ______________________________________

Name ____________________

"Tracking the Tracks to the Brush"

Sam shuts his eyes and drums his hand on his bill. He has a bigger mystery than the one by the tracks.

What makes little wet tracks on the sill and on the rug?

A plan struck Sam.
He can brush the tracks with sand so the tracks stand out.

Then he can track the little sandy tracks.

The tracks go up to the Shutterbug Club, but the club is shut.

Sam sees the tracks go to the brush.
Yuck! Is it a bug or a grub?

No, it is a band of slugs! One is thin. One is fatter, and the biggest one makes the fattest tracks.

Sam sees them with his own eyes! Can he stop them from getting in?

He will not slug the slugs, but he will shut the sill so they cannot get in. Sam was happy. The case was shut.

Time taken:

2nd reading ____________ 2nd reading ____________ 3rd reading ____________

Name ______________________

Opposites

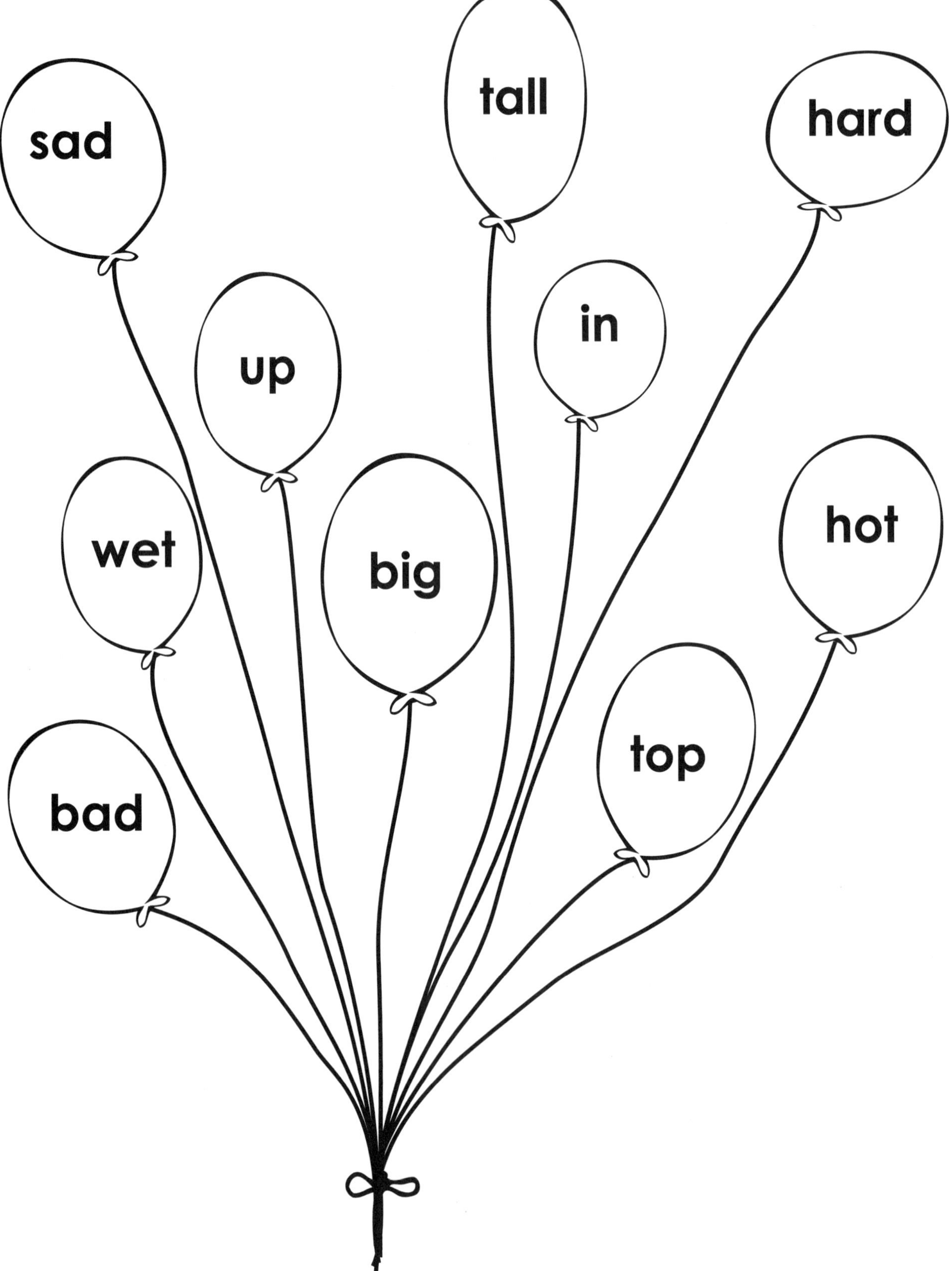

Name ______________________

RAN Chart (Core Words)

brush	club	drum	grub
slug	struck	grub	brush
club	slug	drum	struck

Time taken:

2nd reading ____________ 2nd reading ____________ 3rd reading ____________

Name ______________________

Dice Are Nice!

Real Words	Non-Words

Name ____________________

"Clubs"

Clubs, clubs, clubs.
Which one is best for you?

The Rubber Ducky Club?
Can you dip in the tub and make the best waves?

The Pickup Truck Club?
Can you pick up the biggest crate and put it in the big truck?

The Slugger Club?
Can you slug the ball and then run for home?

The Drum Club?
Can you drum the saddest note on the drum with the sticks?

The Shutterbug Club?
Can you take the hottest shots of the animals and the kids?

The Lucky Puck Club?
Can you use the thinnest stick and the biggest puck?

The Slam-Dunk Club?
Are you the fittest one?
Can you run, jump, and dunk the ball?

Clubs, clubs, clubs.
Which one is best for you?

Time taken:

2nd reading ____________ 2nd reading ____________ 3rd reading ____________

Name ______________________

Rime Family Words

Real Words	Non-Words

Name ____________________

RAN Chart (Core Words + Review)

brush	use	spin	struck
slug	fine	grub	trap
cone	drum	stand	club

Time taken:

2nd reading ____________ 2nd reading ____________ 3rd reading ____________

Name ___________________

"Bones"

The bones inside your body give you your shape.

Tap the top of your body. The bone you tapped is your skull. The skull makes your brain safe.

Poke your back. You have a backbone there. It is called your spine. It is made from 26 bones in the shape of little tubes. The spine bones let you stand, tip, or dip.

Your hand has 27 bones! You can dig, wave, or clap with your hands.

Tap on your chest. The bones in your chest are your ribs. You have 24 rib bones and your lungs are inside them. Air goes in and out of the lungs.

Tap your hip bones. They fit with the spine so that you can wag and shake them. Legs fit with the hips so that you can kick, skip, hop, and run. Shake a hip and a leg!

You have lots of bones. When you are a little kid, you have 300 bones. But as you get bigger, you will have 206 bones. Why is that? As you get bigger, the bones fuse!

Time taken:

2nd reading ___________ 2nd reading ___________ 3rd reading ___________

Name ____________________

Read and Draw Worksheet

Draw pictures to show one of these sentences.

1. I am sad. Bill is sadder. Mike is the saddest.
2. My plant is tall, Bob's is taller, but Kate has the tallest one.
3. My cat is sad. Jake's cat is sadder, but Bob's cat is the saddest.
4. My flapjack is flat, Tim's is flatter, but Sam's is the flattest.

Name ______________________

RAVE-O Phrases

1. ____

2. ____

3. ____

4. ____

5. ____

6. ____

Name ____________________

Sam Sleuth Words

1.	
2.	
3.	
4.	
5.	
6.	

Name ______________________

Create *block*

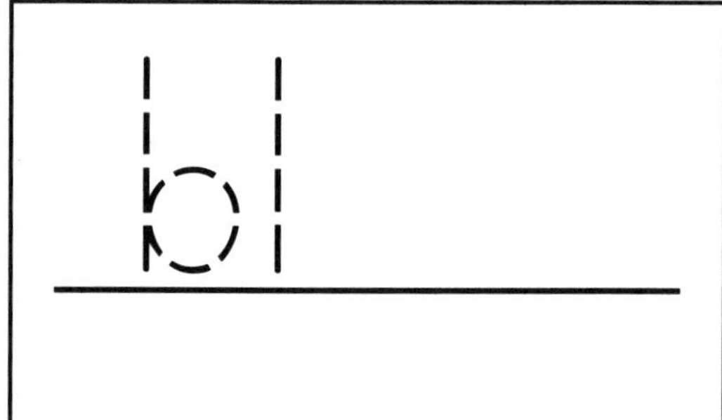

15.1.f

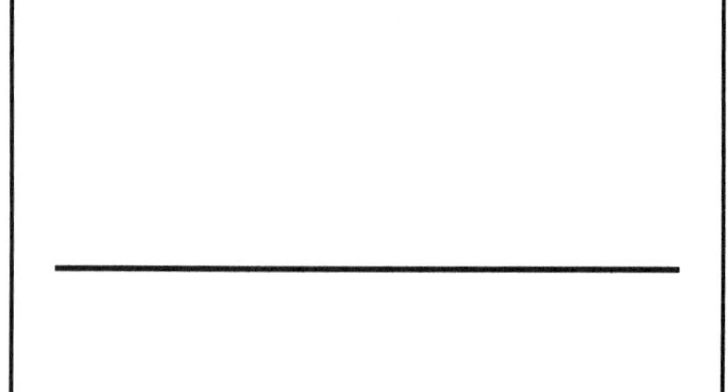

15.1.d

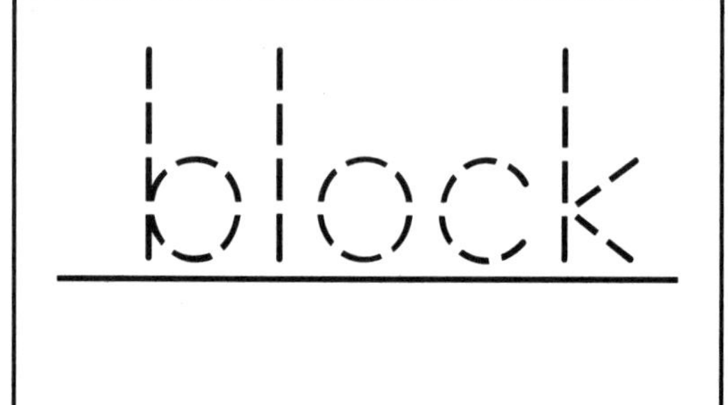

15.1.b

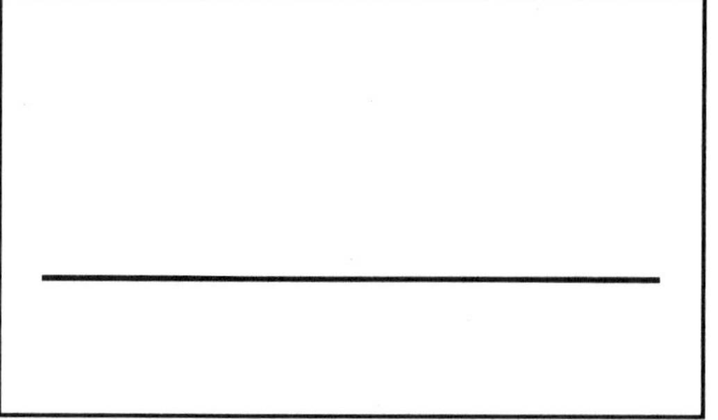

You must put on sun ______________!

Name ____________________

Dictated Sentences *block* and *blip*

1. ____

____

2. ____

____

3. ____

____

UNIT 15

Name ____________________

Create *plot*

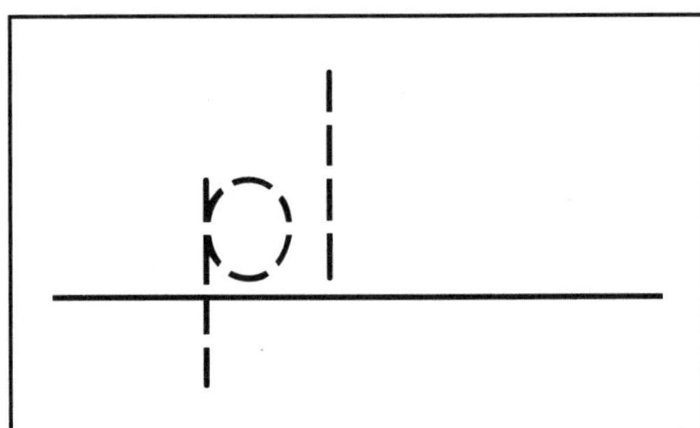

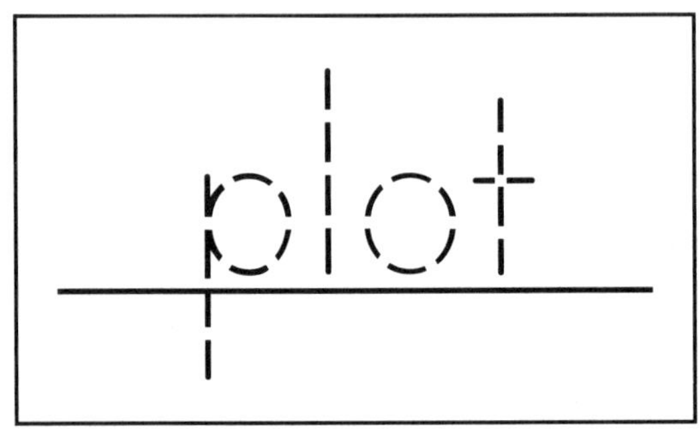

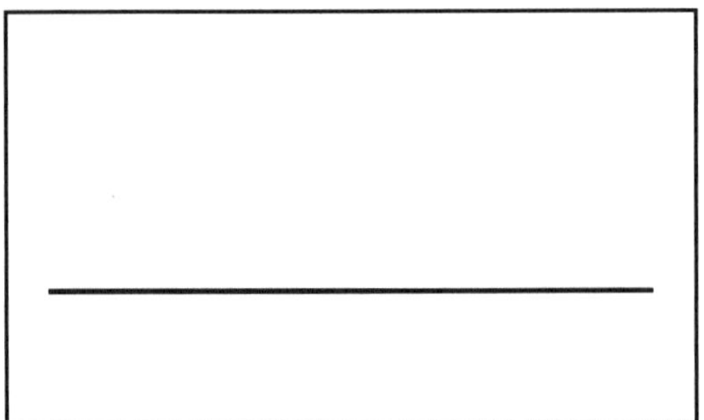

Chip likes the funny ____________.

Name ____________________

Dictated Sentences *plot* and *plane*

1. ____

____

2. ____

____

3. ____

____

Name ______________________

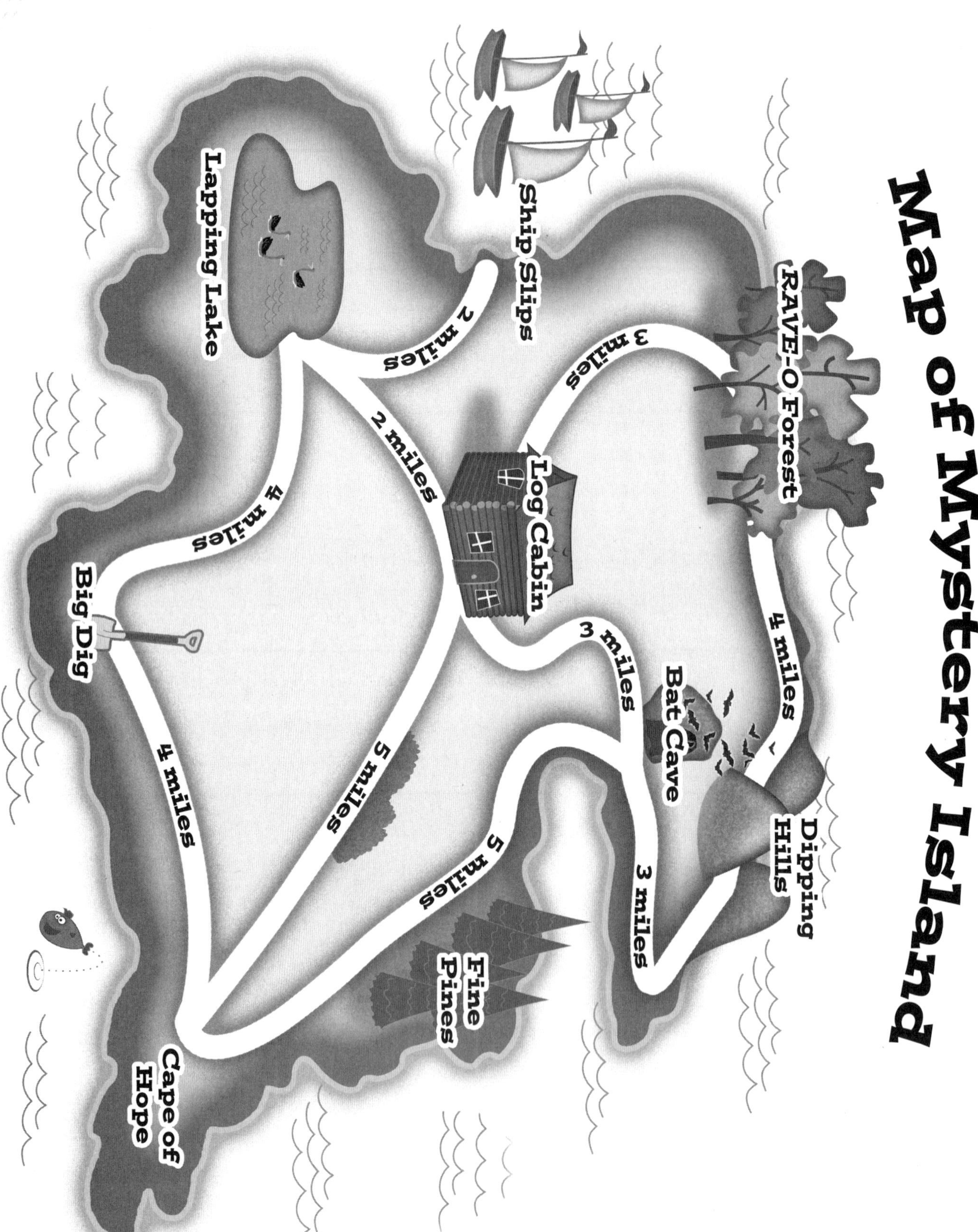
Map of Mystery Island
RAVE-O Forest
Ship Slips
Lapping Lake
Log Cabin
Bat Cave
Dipping Hills
Big Dig
Fine Pines
Cape of Hope
2 miles
3 miles
2 miles
4 miles
4 miles
3 miles
4 miles
5 miles
5 miles
3 miles

Name ______________________

Similarities and Differences

Look at the two words in each example and write how they are alike and how they are different.

bat **fish**

Alike ______________________________________

Different ___________________________________

• •

dollar bill **dime**

Alike ______________________________________

Different ___________________________________

• •

bag **backpack**

Alike ______________________________________

Different ___________________________________

Name ____________________

Mystery Island

Character Description

Choose a name for your character and three words to describe what he/she is like. Write the words in the blanks in the first sentence. Write more information about your character in the space below.

____________________ is ____________________, ____________________,
(character's name)

and ____________________.

____

____

____

____

____

Name ______________________

Create *shop*

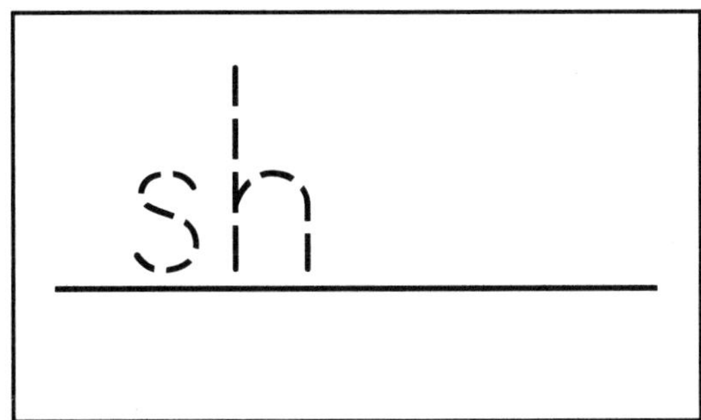

15.3.a

15.3.b

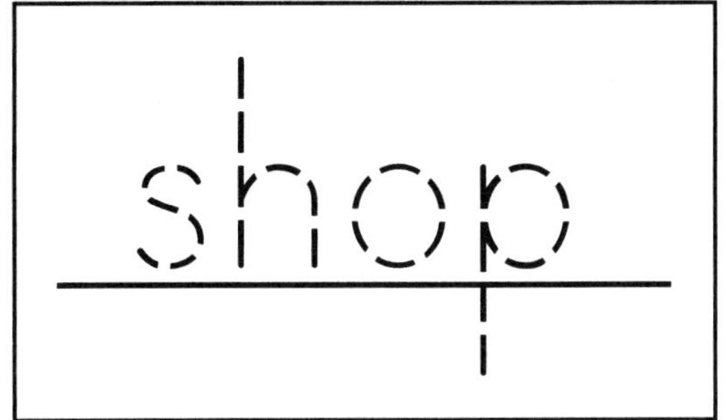

15.3.c

Pat cuts logs in her ______________.

Name ______________________

Dictated Sentences *shop* and *shock*

1. ____

____

2. ____

____

3. ____

____

Name ______________________

Create *chop*

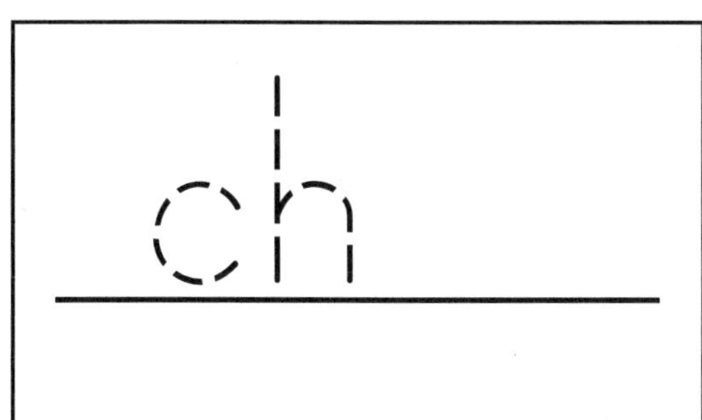

15.4.c

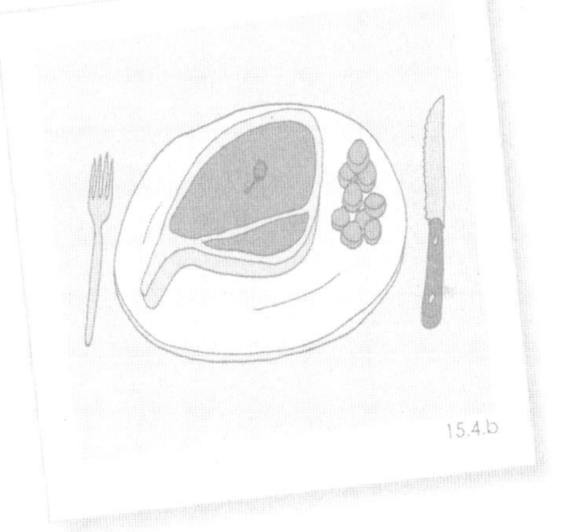

15.4.b

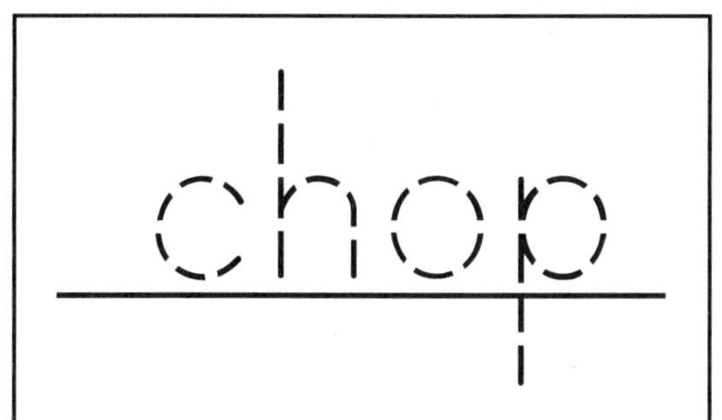

15.4.d

Dan and Jack ___________ the logs.

Name ______________________

Dictated Phrases *chop* and *chick*

1. ____

____

2. ____

____

3. ____

____

Name ______________________

Add Ender Bender *y*

1. The day is ______________ and ______________.
(sun) (gust)

2. My hand is ______________ and ______________.
(clam) (grub)

3. My hat is ______________ and ______________.
(flop) (frill)

4. My cake is ______________ and ______________.
(crust) (nut)

5. The land is ______________ and ______________.
(hill) (sand)

6. My cat is ______________ and ______________.
(skin) (sill)

Time taken:

2nd reading ____________ 2nd reading ____________ 3rd reading ____________

Name ______________________

Mystery Island

Problem Identification

As a class, discuss the main problem in your Mystery Island story. Write *your* idea for the problem in the space below.

The problem in the story "Mystery Island" is:

____

____

____

____

____

____

____

Name ______________________

Create *frog*

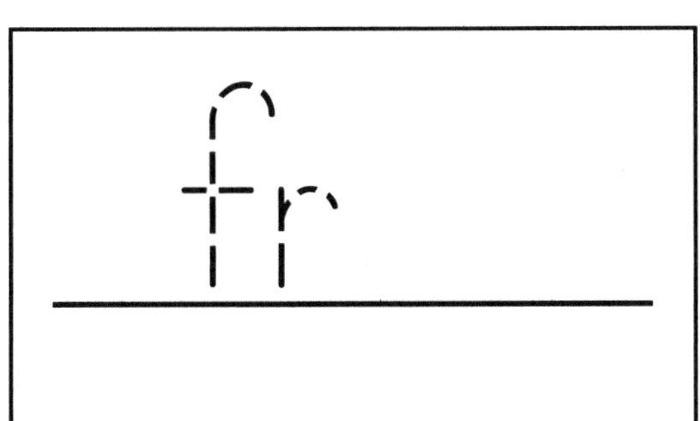

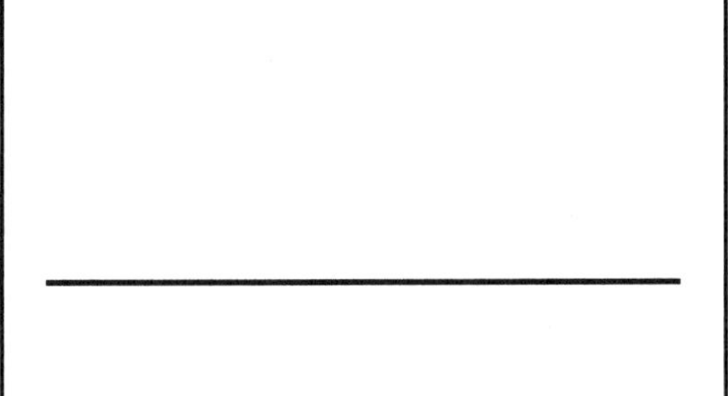

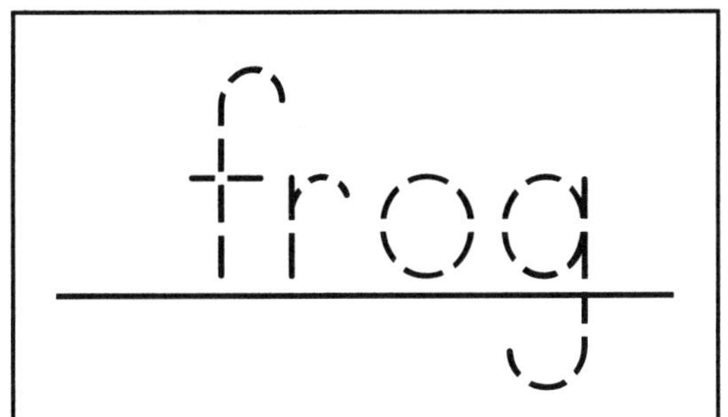

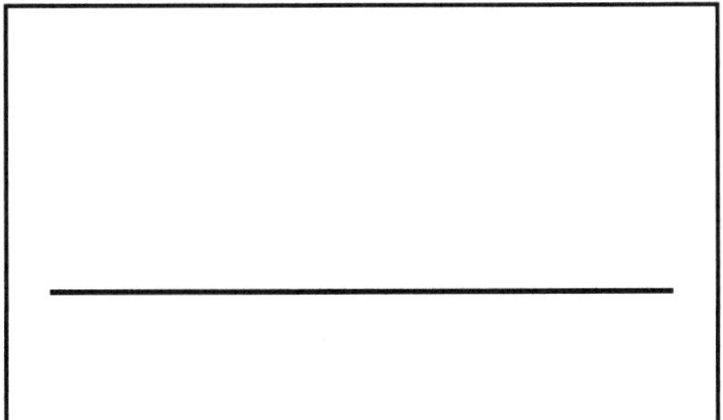

The ______________ hops on the log.

Name ______________________

Dictated Phrases *frog* and *frill*

1. ____

____

2. ____

____

3. ____

____

Name ______________________

Eye-Spy Words

Units 2–9

the	do	I	get	that	when	as
is	on	are	from	me	why	them
in	not	of	what	out	where	go
a	see	he	my	but	who	they
this	at	by	was	so	how	here
and	it	with	little	Mom	very	there
has	she	for	him	then	water	
	his	to	we	up	says	
	happy	said	if		you	
					no	

Units 10–15

wants	saw	which
have	yes	animals
her	be	give
make	mystery	brain
like	home	air
all	magic	goes
off	put	lungs
were	eye	body
wink	one	
your	own	

Name ______________________

"The Frog on the Block!"

Kate's home is on this block.

Kate goes into the shop at the top of the block. It sells lots of things.

A little frog from the bog hops up the block.

Hip-hop. The little frog goes into the shop, too.

Hip-hop. The frog hops on the chops.

Kate sees the frog on the chops in the shop and puts the frog in her bag.

The little frog hops out of the bag and hops to the back of the shop.

A man is chopping logs at the back of the shop.

The frog hops onto the log that the man is chopping at the back of the shop at the top of the block.

STOP!
I do not like this plot.
I do not like this block!
I want to go back to my log in the bog!

Time taken:

2nd reading ____________ 2nd reading ____________ 3rd reading ____________

Name ____________________

"The Chopper"

Bobby Hopper has a wide grin.
His job is to drive a chopper.

Bobby plans trips in his chopper. He plots them on a map. Bobby is a big shot, but if the chopper stops, he will not make a dime!

The chopper stopped!

The chopper is on the block in the shop. The man in the van is there in the shop.
He hops onto the top of the chopper.

"The chopper is not shot," said the man. "The fan is clogged with grape jam, not with grime!"
"I am shocked," said Bobby. "It must be a plot!"

The man unclogs the fan.
The chopper is running tip-top.
Bobby grins, "You are the tops!
You got me out of a sticky jam!"

The man grins back. "I have had my own jams. I like to do for you what Zapcat did for me."

Time taken:

2nd reading ____________ 2nd reading ____________ 3rd reading ____________

Name ______________________

Change *y* to *i* and Add Ender Benders *er* and *est*

The letter ***y*** is bold in the word so you can see which letter that will change. Fill in the spaces with the correct words.

Luck**y** me! Matt is ________________ than Bob, but I am the ________________ one.

The land is rock**y** here. It is ________________ there, but it is not the ________________ in the land.

This chip is nutt**y**. Lots of chips are ________________, but this is the ________________ one of all.

My cat is grubb**y**. She cannot get ________________. She is the ________________ cat.

Name ___________________________

RAN Chart (Core Words)

chop	frog	plot	block
shop	frog	chop	shop
frog	chop	block	shop

Time taken:

2nd reading ______________ 2nd reading ______________ 3rd reading ______________

UNIT 15

Name ______________________

Rime Family Words

Real Words	Non-Words

UNIT 15 Name ___________________________

"Tadpoles to Frogs"

Frogs lay eggs in water. Frogs' eggs are called frogspawn. Frogspawn is like jelly with dots in it. The dots are the little frogs that are called tadpoles.

The tadpoles get out of the jelly and grip plants in the water. They have gills so that they can get air from the water like fish do.

When they get bigger, they have no gills. They have lungs to get air. The tadpoles have tails to swim in the water.

The tadpoles get two back legs and then two at the front. Then the tails go!

They are frogs! They can hop and jump. They get out of the water and into the air.

They sit by the side of lakes, swim in the water, and get bugs for dinner.

The big frogs get bigger, and one day they too will lay eggs in the water.

Time taken:

2nd reading ____________ 2nd reading ____________ 3rd reading ____________

Name ____________________

Sentence Combining

lay in the water Frogs little eggs

1. ____________________

a wide grin has and black eyes Bobby

2. ____________________

on the block into the big shop goes The happy frog

3. ____________________

chops The tall man with a small chopper the bumpy log

4. ____________________

Name ______________________

RAN Chart (Core Words + Review)

chop	brush	pine	flat
cone	shop	struck	frog
plot	drum	block	stand

Time taken:

2nd reading ____________ 2nd reading ____________ 3rd reading ____________

Name ____________________

Categories Worksheet

Animals	Foods

Name ____________________

Nonsense Sentences

Underline the word in each sentence that does not make sense. Circle the incorrect letter and write the correct word in the blank next to the sentence.

1. When I ran home, my logs were fine. ______________
2. Kim slapped on the wet track. ______________
3. The van brushed the ship's deck. ______________
4. They made a trip for the animals. ______________
5. The man hit the drum with a stuck. ______________
6. The pat is out of the bag! ______________
7. Water calls from my eyes. ______________
8. The ship was a check! ______________
9. I well have the grape jam. ______________
10. Which trick is better to run on? ______________

Name ______________________

Create *step*

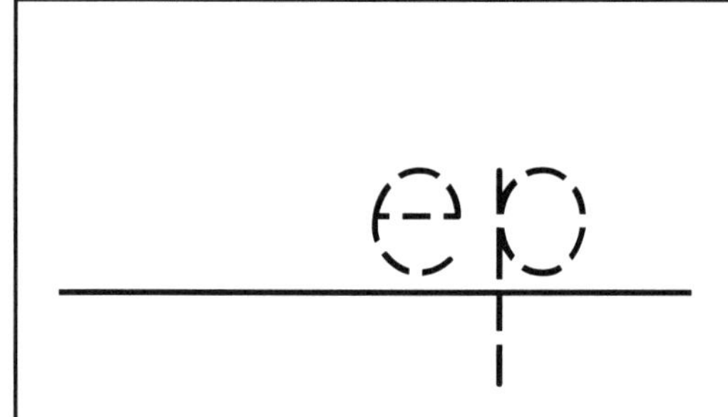

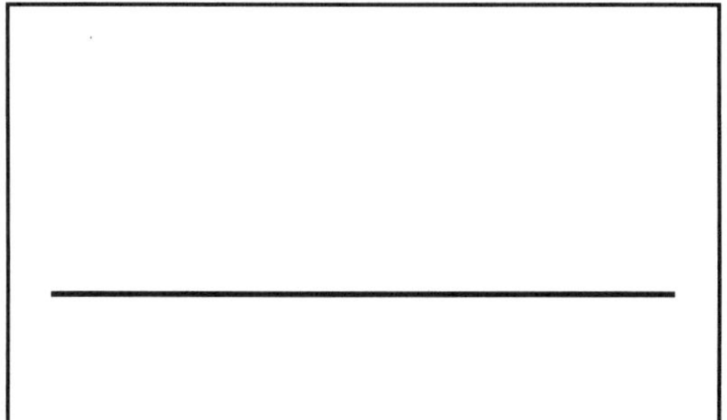

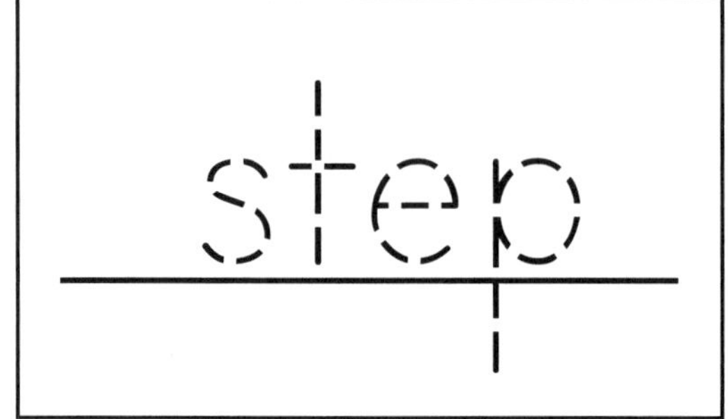

That is a big ______________.

Name ______________________

Dictated Sentences *step* and *pep*

1. ____

____

2. ____

____

3. ____

____

Name ______________________

Create *spell*

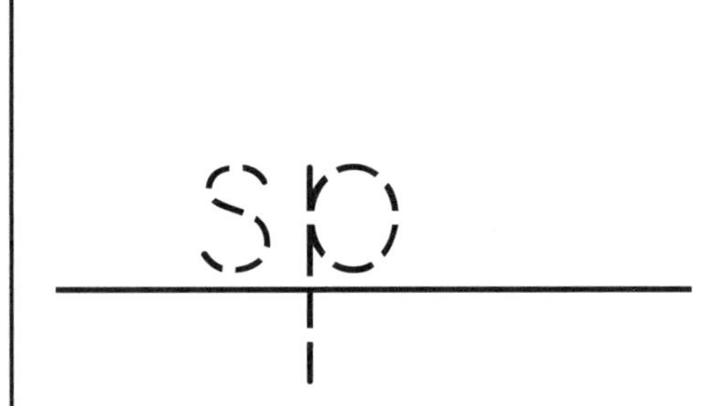

16.2.a

16.2.b

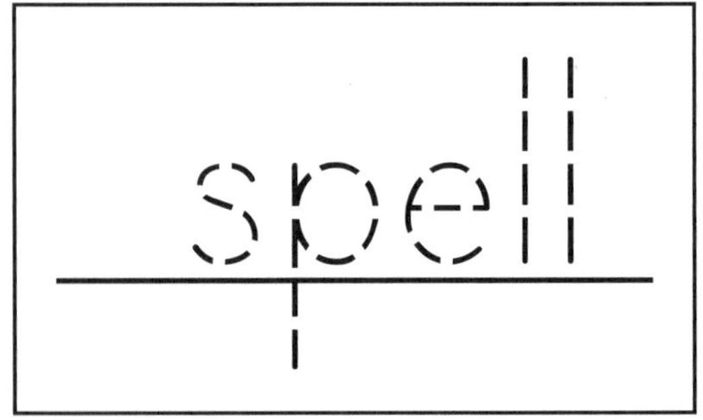

16.2.c

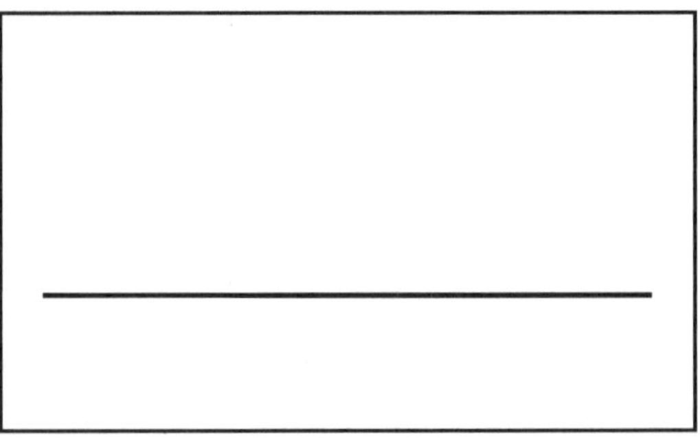

Does Ben ______________ well?

Name ___________________

Dictated Phrases *spell, fell,* and *spot*

1. ______________________________________

____

2. ______________________________________

____

3. ______________________________________

____

Name ______________________

Create *check*

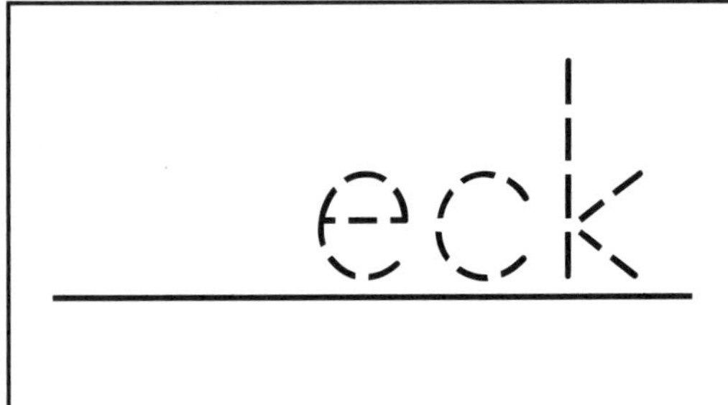

16.3.e

16.3.a

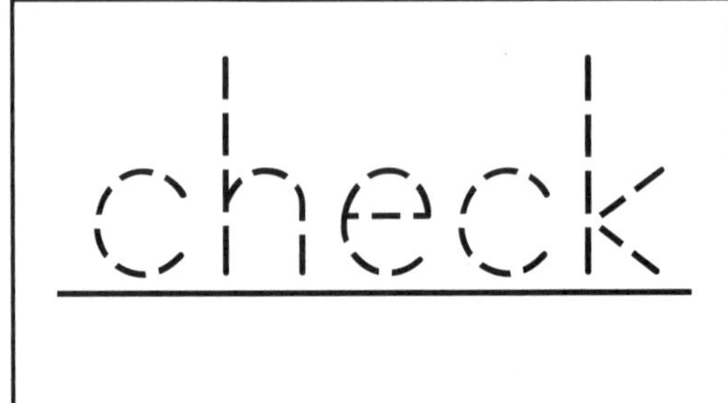

16.3.c

Did Nate ______________ all the steps?

Name ____________________

Create *wreck*

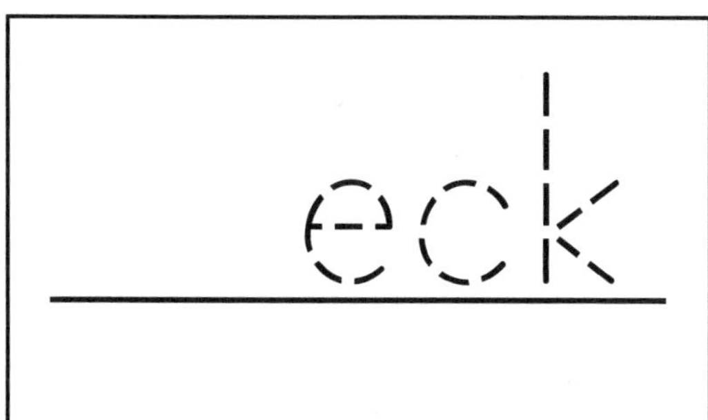

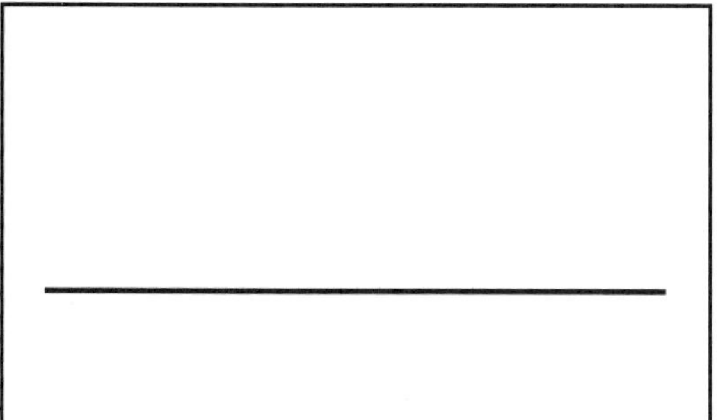

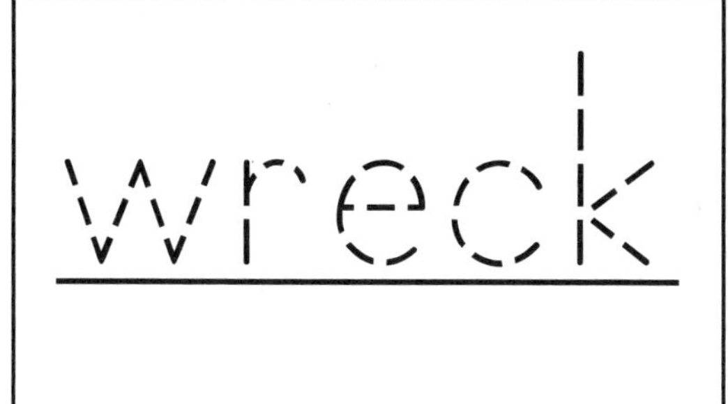

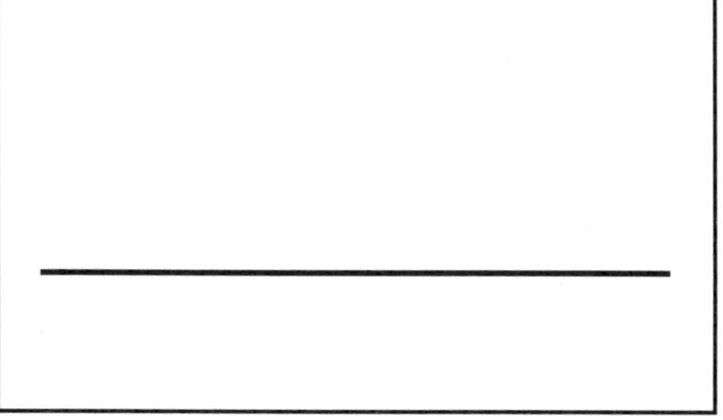

Your locker is a ____________________!

Name ____________________

Dictated Sentences *check* and *wreck*

1. ______________________________

____

2. ______________________________

____

3. ______________________________

____

UNIT 16

Name ______________________

Eye-Spy Words

Units 2–9

the	do	I	get	that	when	as
is	on	are	from	me	why	them
in	not	of	what	out	where	go
a	see	he	my	but	who	they
this	at	by	was	so	how	here
and	it	with	little	Mom	very	there
has	she	for	him	then	water	
	his	to	we	up	says	
	happy	said	if		you	
					no	

Units 10–16

wants	saw	which	spawn
have	yes	animals	front
her	be	give	two
make	mystery	brain	tail
like	home	air	
all	magic	goes	
off	put	lungs	
were	eye	body	
wink	one	too	
your	own	thing	

Name ______________________

"What Is in the Cave?"
Chapter 1

Bob and Kim like to go on bike rides in the hills. They plan to ride to a cave in the hillside by the sea.

They get to a wide sandbank and put the bikes in the shade. They take a rope with them. They fix it to a rock at the front of the cave. The rocky slope into the cave is so slippery that they slide to one side. They cling to the rope to be safe.

The cave is dim. Only a thin ray of sun is trapped in there. Bob and Kim do not want to be trapped, but they want to see what is in the cave.

Bob's leg hits what he thinks is a big stone. In the sun's thin ray, they can see it is not a stone but a chest with a rusty padlock!

Time taken:

2nd reading ____________ 2nd reading ____________ 3rd reading ____________

Name ___________________

"What Is in the Cave?"
Chapter 2

Bob checks the padlock. He taps it with a stone, and the lock opens. Inside is a very big cup.

"What can it be?" says Kim. "Let me take it outside."

Just then, Kim sees black things shake at the top of the cave.

"Yikes! There are bats in this cave!" she says in a hushed tone. "They are not awake in the daytime, but it is getting late. They are awake now! Let us get out!"

Kim grabs the cup, and they backtrack out of the cave.

The bats wake up and flit out of the cave, too. Bob and Kim stand still. They are stuck as the bats rush out, brushing by them. The bats want bugs, not Bob and Kim, but Kim shakes and shakes. The cup slips and drops outside the cave onto the rocks! What a blow!

Time taken:

2nd reading ____________ 2nd reading ____________ 3rd reading ____________

Name ______________________

"What Is in the Cave?"
Chapter 3

Bob runs out of the cave onto the hillside. He cannot see the cup. It is lost in the rocks and sand.

"I am a wreck," says Kim. "Bats and I do not mix."

Bob says, "How can we get the cup back? We will not see it if the sun sets."

A thin ray of the sun hits the cup, and they see it shine in the rocks by the sea.

"What luck," says Bob, and he runs to get it.

Bob picks up the cup and says, "Wow! This cup is made of copper and jade! There is a date on it, too."

He rubs the cup and sees the date '1768.'

"I bet this cup came from a shipwreck in 1768!" Bob says. "We can take it home in my backpack."

"If this was in the cave, do you think there are . . ." Kim stops! Her eyes open wide! She shakes! She sees a white, shadowy shape by the chest. What IS in that cave?

Time taken:

2nd reading ____________ 2nd reading ____________ 3rd reading ____________

Name ______________________

e__ Rime Family Words

1.		9.	
2.		10.	
3.		11.	
4.		12.	
5.		13.	
6.		14.	
7.		15.	
8.		16.	

Name ______________________

wr Words

wrap

wreck

wren

wrote

write

Name ______________________

Fatrat Sentences Worksheet

1. The tomcat ate the catfish.
2. The shipwreck upset the shellfish.
3. I like cupcakes and pancakes.
4. The job is at a standstill.
5. wishbone drumstick

____

____

6. sandbox swingset

____

____

7. butterfly rosebush

____

____

8. workbook backpack

____

____

Name ______________________

RAN Chart (Core Words)

check	spell	step	wreck
spell	check	wreck	step
check	wreck	step	spell

Time taken:

2nd reading ____________ 2nd reading ____________ 3rd reading ____________

Name ____________________

"Stump the Pros" Game

Real Words	Non-Words

Name ______________________

RAN Chart (Core Words + Review)

plot	drum	spin	stand
trap	block	step	brush
chop	wreck	spell	track
trim	flat	check	club

Time taken:

2nd reading ____________ 2nd reading ____________ 3rd reading ____________

Name ______________________

Ender Bender Words

wreck
wrecking
wrecked
wrecker
wrecks
wrapping
wringing
wrings

spell
spelling
speller
spells
spilled
spilling
spotting
spotty

checker
checkers
checked
checking
chicks
chicken
choppy
chilly

step
stepping
stepped
stopped
stopping
sticky
stocky
steps

UNIT 16 Name ______________________

Completed Word Wall

pad	crab	kick		bob	rub	deck	cane
tag		kid		lock	club	check	cape
jam	track	dig		rock	grub	wreck	date
ham		pig		block	duck	bed	fine
ram		bill	trim	frog	struck	leg	pine
can	stand	pin	spin	top	bug	well	cone
fan	plan	dip	chip	pop	slug	spell	note
cap	trap	skip	ship	chop	drum	pen	cube
lap		tip	slip	shop	run	pet	tube
tap		fish		pot	brush	step	use
bat	flat	bit		plot	just		
pat					nut		

Time taken:

2nd reading ____________ 2nd reading ____________ 3rd reading ____________

Name ______________________

Rime Family Words
Consolidation Day 1

Real Words	Non-Words

Name ______________________

All About Nouns and Verbs

Nouns

Finish this sentence and then write the words in the columns. Fill up ar
spaces with your own words.

Nouns can be ______________________

Chip	well	tube	they	bat	Tim
block	cap	she	shop	he	home
stand	Mack	plan	cane	I	Jim

People	Pronouns	Places	Things

Verbs

Finish this sentence and then fill up the spaces in the columns with you
own words.

Verbs are ______________________

Verbs	Verbs With *s*	Verbs With *ed*	Verbs With *er*	Verbs With *in*

Name ____________________

Simple Sentences

Highlight all nouns in one color and all verbs in another color.

1. Bill sits.
2. Dan chats.
3. Trish runs.
4. Jack tracks the frog.
5. Jill and Bob fish.
6. Kim checks the spellings.
7. Pam and Pat struck the drum.
8. Sam locked the locker.
9. Jane slipped the note in the pad.
10. The batter batted with the bat.
11. Mike patted the dog and slipped the tag on its neck.
12. The duck, the ram, and the kid pined for the pines.

Name ______________________

Eye-Spy Words

the	by	then	her	give
is	with	up	make	brain
in	for	when	like	air
a	to	why	all	goes
this	said	where	off	lungs
and	get	who	were	body
has	from	how	wink	too
do	what	very	your	thing
on	my	water	saw	spawn
not	was	says	yes	front
see	little	you	be	two
at	him	no	mystery	tail
it	we	as	home	sea
she	if	them	magic	only
his	that	go	put	us
happy	me	they	eye	blow
I	out	here	one	now
are	but	there	own	
of	so	wants	which	
he	Mom	have	animals	

Name ______________________

Rime Family Words
Consolidation Day 2

Real Words	Non-Words

Name ______________________

Ender Benders *s* and *ing*

Ender Bender Words: ***tap, rock, trim, plot, fish, spin***

Ender Bender Sentences:

1. ______________________

____

2. ______________________

____

Name ___________________________

Sentences Worksheet

1. I am jamming the bat and the cape in the bag so that I can lock it.

2. Dan and Sam are kicking and skipping and tapping on the big drum.

3. The kid is pinning a big fish pin on Sam's cap.

4. I am patting a dog that is slipping his pad on my leg and is checking for tidbits.

5. Matt dips the chip in the dip, pops the lid of the can, and sips the water.

6. We are brushing the deck and tipping the sand in the rocks by the crab tracks.

My sentence:

____

____

____

Name ______________________

Vowels Worksheet

UNIT 16

Name ____________________

Rime Family Words
Consolidation Day 3

Real Words	Non-Words

UNIT 16

Name ______________________

Ender Bender *ed*

Ender Bender *ed* Words:

Ender Bender Sentence:

____

____

Name ______________________

Add Describers

Nouns:	Describers:
fish	
note	
club	
rock	

Sentences:

Name ____________________

Transform Words

	⇨	
	⇨	
	⇨	
	⇨	
	⇨	
	⇨	
	⇨	
	⇨	

Name ______________________

Ender Bender *er*

sadder	potter	taller	madder	winner	slimmer
bigger	banner	wrapper	batter	flatter	drummer
shutter	bidder	spinner	flipper	hotter	copper

More	Person	New Meaning

 Name ______________________

"Nate's Note"

Nate woke up and saw a note on his bed. The note said,

Hi Nate,
I am one of your pals.
Can you tell who I am?
I like cupcakes, napping, and sledding.
I do not like grapes or pets.
Your mystery pal.

Nate grabbed a cap, and went out to track his pen pal. Nate rushed out the gate to see his pal Jake.

"Checkers and I made cupcakes," said Jake. "Checkers is my pet dog and sidekick! He and I like hot cupcakes."

Can Jake be the mystery pal? No? Why?

Nate ate a cupcake and grabbed one to go as he said, "See you!" to Jake.
Nate jogged to Kate's home. Kate was napping.

"Hi Nate," she said. "I am groggy, so I must take a nap. Have some of my red grapes."

Can Kate be the mystery pal? No? Why?

The shades were blocking the sun. Nate let Kate take her nap.

Name ______________________

Outside, Nate saw Kenny. Kenny was upset.

"I was napping on that rock and I fell and struck my leg," he sobbed. "I cannot go on my sled."

Nate said, "Do you want a cupcake and some grapes?"

"I will just have the cupcake," said Kenny. "But how can I go on my sled with a bad leg?"

"You can wrap it in my wrap!" said Nate. "I will be back."

Nate ran home to get the wrap for Kenny's leg. He picked up the wrap and saw the note.

Nate checked the mixed-up note. Can you tell Nate who wrote the note?

Just then, it struck him! He jogged back to Kenny.

"You are my pen pal. You wrote that note!" said Nate.

"Yes, I did," Kenny nodded. "You are a tip-top tracker, Nate."

Nate wrapped up Kenny's leg, and they sledded till sunset.

Time taken:

2nd reading ____________ 2nd reading ____________ 3rd reading ____________

Name ____________________

"Nate's Note" Questions Worksheet

1. Who is the main character? ____________________

____

ɔmplete sentences to answer the questions below.

ᵗ is the problem in this story? ____________________

____

____

3. How does Nate know that Jake is not his pen pal? ____________________

____

4. How does Nate know that Kate is not his pen pal? ____________________

____

5. How is the problem solved? ____________________

____

6. What does Kenny mean when he calls Nate a "tip-top tracker"?

____

____

7. What are the three parts of Think Thrice? ____________________

____

Name ______________________

Sentence Builders Worksheet

My nouns and pronouns are [ ]

My verbs and helping verbs are [ ]

My describers are [ ]

My prepositions are [ ]

Nate grabbed a big cap and went out the door.

Jake and Checkers made hot cupcakes on the deck.

Kate was taking a nap in her bed.

Kenny had a bad leg. He hit his leg on a rock.

Nate saw the mystery note on his bed.

Name ______________________

Change Ender Bender *y* to *ier* and *iest*

EXAMPLES: **sand** **sandy** **sandier** **sandiest**

My dog is sandy.

My dog is sandier than yours.

My dog is the sandiest dog of all.

Choose one of the words from the list below and add Ender Benders ***y***, ***ier***, and ***iest*** to make three new words. Write a sentence using each new word, like the sentences in the example above.

rust **wit** **trick** **flop**

1. ______________________________

2. ______________________________

3. ______________________________

Use one of your own words, or choose another word from the list, and make three more sentences.

1. ______________________________

2. ______________________________

3. ______________________________

Name ______________________

Sentence Completion

1. He ________________ a big sack of yams and figs.

2. Jim and Pam ________________ with the little kids.

3. Jan ______________ the tin can and it ______________ the tip of the rock.

4. Chip ________________ the tag on the man in the van.

5. Zack ________________ the dust on the deck.

6. They ________________ the tracks of the dog in the pines.

Verb Bank

are kidding	brushed	hits
pinned	slipped	kicks
is dragging	are tracking